I Am Presence
and
Violet Flame

bj King

1st WORLD
PUBLISHING

I Am Presence and Violet Flame

bj King

Copyright © 2025 by bj King

Published by 1st World Publishing
P.O. Box 2211, Fairfield, Iowa 52556
tel: 641-209-5000 • fax: 866-440-5234
web: www.1stworldpublishing.com

First Edition
ISBN Softcover: 978-1-4218-3589-1
LCCN: Library of Congress Cataloging-in-Publication Data

This material has been written and published for educational purposes to enhance one's well-being. In regard to health issues, the information is not intended as a substitute for appropriate care and advice from health professionals, nor does it equate to the assumption of medical or any other form of liability on the part of the publisher or author. The publisher and author shall have neither liability nor responsibility to any person or entity with respect to loss, damages, or injury claimed to be caused directly or indirectly by any information in this book.

What I offer to you in this book are my own opinions and beliefs based on direct experiences with Spirit over the past thirty-eight years and information I've consolidated from reading Ancient Wisdom teachings. These statements are not presented as THE TRUTH. Do not accept what I have written as truth only as one person's opinion. Accept only what resonates with your own discernment, your own truth. Discernment is one of the spiritual gifts promised to us all. If you do not feel you have it, pray for it. All spiritual gifts are given to us as a result of our asking for them. How you utilize the information in this book you do at your own risk, I accept no responsibility.

This book is dedicated to Shelagh Schopen,
who created the I AM Chart
and the amazing deck of the 49 Rays of God cards,
with my eternal gratitude and Love,
bj

Table of Contents

1.

How I Became Aware of the I Am Presence

HAWAII, MET GEORGIA O'KEEFE AND SURVIVED CANCER

I began receiving messages from my soul September 30, 1982. Before that time I knew nothing of the Spiritual Hierarchy, the Ascended Masters, the Intergalactic Federation, or Angels. Through the years these things were revealed to me in meditation and became an obvious and real part of my daily life.

At the request of my soul in 1985, I sold my belongings and began to travel. Each day Spirit would indicate, during my meditation, what city they wished for me to travel to and gave me names of people I was to locate. These people were either people I was to deliver messages to from their souls, or they were people Spirit expected to take care of me for a few days until my next assignment was revealed in meditation.

I traveled first to Denver, CO to reconnect with a longtime friend. I explained to her and to her husband how the communication with my soul had started through meditation and what I was being expected to do. At first they were hesitant, but were very willing to put me up for a few days. The woman, after sleeping on the idea, admitted to me that if she had heard this story from anyone else she would have dismissed that person as crazy, but coming from me she had to take what I was saying seriously, because she knew me to be an honest and sane person. During my time in Denver I met a woman who was also a channel. She wanted to exchange soul readings with me. During my reading she told me about the Spiritual Hierarchy and about her work with them. She said that my soul was saying that I would eventually work with the Hierarchy on a daily basis and especially work closely with the Master Saint Germain and the Master Jesus. She said I would become one of the primary channels for Saint Germain at a future time.

She explained that Saint Germain is an Ascended Master and the Master of the Seventh Ray and the Violet Flame of Transformation. She said he works with the Arch Angel Zadkiel and his Divine Complement is Ascended Master Lady Portia. She could have just as well been speaking a foreign language as far as I was concerned, because I did not understand the significance of what she was saying.

I thought, "This woman is crazy. She's trying to either scare me or impress me. I don't believe any of what she's saying." But I kept a "nice people" smile on my face and thanked her for her time and the information. Shortly thereafter, I became aware of Elizabeth Clare Prophet and the Summit Lighthouse group in California. She was at that time considered the primary channel for Saint Germain, the Spiritual Hierarchy and the teachings of the "I AM." I became aware of H. P. Blavatsky and the books she had channeled from the Masters called *Isis Unveiled* and *The Secret Doctrine* books. I heard of a set of blue books channeled from the Hierarchy by a woman named Alice Bailey. I did not own any of these books. I also became aware that there were people in the village of Mt. Shasta, CA who taught about the "I AM Presence." I was told that on the second Sunday in August this group held what was called the "I AM Pageant," a play reenacting, not the crucifixion but the ascension of Christ and that the pageant depicted the miracles of Jesus and the teachings of His ministry. I was intrigued.

After leaving Denver I went to Portland, OR where I met a man. We had a great week together. The next weekend, when Spirit had suggested I drive on down to Mt, Shasta to attend the "I AM Pageant—A Pageant on the Life of Beloved Jesus the Christ," I stayed in Oregon instead to spend the weekend at the Oregon Coast with this man. On Monday I felt guilty that I had not followed the suggestion of Spirit to go on to Mt. Shasta to attend the pageant. I left Oregon and drove on to Mt. Shasta. I had been given the name of a German man who had written a book about the Great White Brotherhood (which is what some people call the Spiritual Hierarchy.) I called him immediately upon arriving in Mt.Shasta, but was unable to connect with him.

I decided to drive up the mountain to meditate to see if I could connect directly with Saint Germain. Legend says that there is a civilization of beings called the Telos, who live inside the mountain and that the mountain was, at that time, the home of the Retreat of Saint Germain. As I drove up the mountain I noticed a hiker, who I thought was a woman because of the long hair. I stopped about half way up the mountain beside a huge flat rock and sat down on the rock to meditate. I was almost immediately connected to the energy of Saint Germain. He asked that when the hiker approached where I was sitting that I was to offer him my sleeping bag, my food and all my money. Needless to say I was confused and scared to follow the directions, because I did not have a place arranged to stay overnight in Mt. Shasta. I had never had to use the sleeping bag, but had always felt safer having it if I ever had to sleep in my car.

When I came out of meditation the man was standing nearby watching me. He was thin, tanned, with long hair and had a long scar down one of his cheeks. I invited him to sit down, which he did. He began to tell me his story. He was hitch-hiking his way cross country from Dallas, Texas where he had lived. He was seeking a vision quest on the mountain to learn his life purpose. He had no food and no money and no blanket and was planning to spend the night on the mountain. The top of the mountain, where he was headed, was still covered with snow. I told him Spirit was instructing me to give him my sleeping bag, food and money. He was amazed, but accepted what was offered, thanked me and walked away.

I got back in my car, even more determined to find the German author who Spirit had said would be responsible for taking care of me. The car would not start! The electrical system was completely dead! The car was new. I had purchased it two months before leaving Oklahoma. I was livid. I felt tricked and confused. I had done what Spirit had asked and now I was stranded. (Being stranded is the only way Spirit could have gotten me to stay in Mt. Shasta for three days.)

Before I left Oklahoma City on my journey, an older neighbor had gifted me with a sun screen that you put in your front window in case of emergency to ask someone to call the police. Immediately after I put the sign in the window a car stopped. The car was driven by an older gentleman who had three female passengers about his own age. They said they had noticed me and the hitch-hiker on their way up the mountain and had been concerned for my safety. The man had a two way radio in his car. These were the days before CB's became popular and many years before car phones and cell phones. His having a two way radio was definitely a miracle. He called for a tow truck and they waited with me until the truck came.

The tow truck took my car to a garage. Now I had no place to stay, no money, one credit card, no food and no transportation. I again called the number I had been given for the German author. This time he answered. I explained to the best of my ability who I was and what I had been told by Spirit. He agreed to come to where I was, which he did, but he was unwilling to take me home with him or to be responsible for me in any way, physically or financially. He did not take me to dinner, but just dropped me off at a small, old motel. I felt discouraged and a bit guilty that I had not arrived in Mt. Shasta over the weekend as Spirit had suggested. I felt my choice to stay in Oregon to have fun had somehow screwed up divine timing.

I went for a walk to try to find a place to eat that would take my credit card. As I was walking along the street I was approached by a very tall, thin, dirty man with dread locks, hiking boots and a walking stick. He asked me what I was doing in Mt. Shasta. I told him it would take more than a minute to explain and that I was looking for a place to have dinner. We went to a café and I told him my story. He mentioned that he had videotaped the "I AM Pageant" and would be glad to hook the VCR to my TV in the motel and show me the whole thing in exchange for the use of my shower. I was pretty leery at first, but got a strong signal from my soul that this was the right thing to do. After dinner I watched the pageant as he showered. Afterward he mentioned that he was planning to go to a meditation group that night and asked if I would like to accompany him. When we arrived, I was amused to find the meditation was at the home of the German author. Our host was shocked and embarrassed by my arrival.

At the end of the evening, the author offered to come and get me the next day and take me up on the mountain to meditate. I assumed he meant that we were going to meditate together. I called about my car the next morning and was appalled to find it would take three days to get the parts to fix it. I was stuck in this unfriendly place for three days. I would have to pay the motel bill for three days and pay for my food. The author picked me up at ten in the morning and we drove up the mountain. When we arrived at a place where a large flat rock spanned the mountain stream we stopped and got out. I sat down to meditate, thinking that he was going to join me, but he said, "I'll be back for you in an hour." Before I could protest he was in his car and gone. I was furious with him and with Spirit. I wanted off this mountain and out of this town, but I was stuck for three days.

I made an effort to calm down enough to meditate. After about ten minutes I made the connection with Saint Germain. He asked me to open my eyes and he stood before me as a Human shaped form made of light. I could not see his features, but the voice inside my head was definitely his. He explained that he had much to teach me about the "I AM Presence" and that if I agreed, he would make himself available to me as a guide. I was overwhelmed, but I agreed. I really had no concept of what that agreement meant.

The author picked me up in exactly one hour. I did not disclose to him what had happened to me on the mountain. We both spoke very little during the drive and he returned me to the motel without even offering to buy me lunch. I never saw him again during the three days I was there. I was never so glad to get my car back and to get out of a place as I was to leave Mt. Shasta. In spite of the wonderful hour I spent with Saint Germain on the mountain, the rest of my stay felt very unfriendly and I intended to never have to return to Mt. Shasta.

Years later, in 1989, I was traveling out of a retreat center outside Charlotte, NC, when I received a message that Spirit needed me to attend a symposium that was going to be held in Ashland, OR. The event was advertised as an Interspecies Interdimensional Symposium. I was told by Spirit that I would be one of the speakers at the symposium. I wondered how that would happen, since I knew none of the people who were responsible for putting on the event, nor did I know any of the presenters. I sent in my registration and bought my ticket all on a credit card and flew to Ashland. During the get acquainted event the night before the symposium was to actually begin, I overheard the chairman of the event explaining to another person that one of the female speakers, who was the most knowledgeable about the Spiritual Hierarchy and the Intergalactic Federation, had just called and cancelled. I walked up to him and introduced myself and offered my services to fill her position. He was astounded, but relieved.

The next morning, the first event involved all the speakers being seated in a row on the platform. We were to introduce ourselves to the audience and tell a little about ourselves and what we would be offering at the symposium. The first speaker stood to speak. He was a man named Frank who explained that he lived in Mt. Shasta and traveled extensively cooperating with the Spiritual Hierarchy and the Federation to do energy work for the planet. I was impressed, since I'd heretofore never met anyone else who did what I was doing. After speaking he sat down. When it came my turn to speak I stood and explained that I am a liaison between the Spiritual Hierarchy, the Federation and the people of Earth. I noticed that while I was speaking, the man named Frank stood up again and was staring at me. He had tears streaming down his face. I was a little embarrassed and did not understand what was happening. He later told me he was moved to tears to hear that someone else was doing what he had been doing with the Hierarchy and the Federation. He had felt very alone in the work he was doing with the Masters.

When I had purchased my ticket to fly to Oregon, Spirit had asked that I arrange to remain in Oregon for two days beyond the close of the symposium. I knew no one in the area so I had no idea what I would be expected to do during those two days. During the two days of the conference, Frank and I taught together about the Federation and the Spiritual Hierarchy, but had no time for personal communication. At the end of the conference, since he was local, he had offered to take people back to the airport. I explained to him that I wouldn't be going to the airport as yet, because I needed to stay in the area for another couple of days. His response was, "Oh, thank goodness. Would you be willing to come to Mt. Shasta for a couple of days and stay at my home so we would have some time to visit?" It is always a relief to me when I get clarity about why I am where I am and that I will have a place to sleep.

A couple of years before I had been sent to a place called Joy Lake outside Reno, NV and I met a man there that I did a reading for. He wanted to move to Mt. Shasta and to open a crystal store. I did not charge him for the reading because it had been my idea. He had not asked for it. I was out of money and needed to drive on to California. I was setting in my car ready to leave, but stopped to meditate before actually starting the car. I heard a tap on the window and it was the man I had read for. He handed me $500 and wished me well in my travels.

As Frank and I drove into Mt. Shasta he said, "I have a friend who has an amazing crystal shop here and if you are not too tired let's stop in and I will introduce you. I've spent thousands of dollars with him." He chuckled as he told me this and I suddenly wondered if it could possibly be the man who had gifted me the $500 and it was. He did not remember me until I reminded him of our meeting.

During that two day period I was with Frank, we talked for hours about our experiences. We became aware that it was Spirit's agenda for me to move to Mt. Shasta and to live with Frank. His home was a beautiful tri-level and had views of Mt. Shasta from every level. At this point in my life, I was exhausted from all the travel and from being homeless. I could not even say the word exhaustion without beginning to cry. I moved to Mt. Shasta in January. Frank took excellent care of me during our time together. We had an agreement that I would remain with him in Mt. Shasta until such time as I received a message from Spirit that it was time to leave. I lived there for exactly nine months.

During the time I lived in Mt. Shasta, my prior to Earth memory returned and I channeled Saint Germain's teachings about the I AM Presence weekly for a small group of Frank's friends. These channeling's were recorded.

September of 1990, I received the message from Spirit that it was time for me to leave Mt. Shasta. I was to leave on the 16th of September by 11 a.m. I did not know where I was headed from there. Frank and I began to pack my car. He was sad to see me leave. I felt much stronger and ready to travel again. While we were packing, I received a call from a couple in New Mexico who offered me their furnished condo rent free for nine months. Once again I knew where I was going.

Between California and New Mexico, Spirit manifested a book in my book boxes that I had not previously owned. The book was the biography of Georgia O'Keeffe. When I unloaded the books I was intrigued to find the book and read it. Georgia was a very accomplished artist who loved New Mexico and flowers. At this point in my life I had not painted large paintings. In fact I wasn't painting much at all since I had sold the bj originals greeting card company in 1985 just before I began to travel.

After a few weeks of being in Albuquerque, I received a call from a woman in Denver who wanted to go to Hawaii for a month to paint and write. She had enough frequent flyer points to buy me a ticket and wanted me to go with her. She rented a cabin at the foot of the mountains in Kauai. The night before we were to leave for Kauai, my body became very distressed. The right side of my body drew up as if I were having a stroke. I had to lie down and could not finish packing. Another friend from Denver was to meet us in Kauai for one week of our month long stay. She called the night before we were to leave to see how I was doing. I explained that I was in severe pain and that my muscles were in spasm on the right side of my body. Kathy is an intuitive person and tuned in to my body.

She asked, "Are the galactic beings you come from slight with small heads?"

"No, they are very tall between six and seven feet tall, some even taller."

"Well, there is a spirit standing beside your bed that is slight and has a small head. She is female."

It suddenly occurred to me that it might be the spirit of Georgia O'Keeffe, since I had been reading her biography. "Ask her if her name is Georgia," I suggested to Kathy.

"She says it is," Kathy offered.

"What does she want?" I demanded.

"She's offering to help you with your painting," Kathy relayed.

I began to cry and to argue for my limitations. I felt totally inadequate to be offered such a gift. I told her that I thought she should help someone who knew how to paint, someone with more talent. Georgia told me through Kathy that she was offering to help artists who knew how to project energy into their work, not people who were technically skilled. "Do you think people want to stare at a painting of bones? I put so much energy into the paintings I gave them no choice but to stare." At this point she chuckled. I gratefully agreed to accept any help she wished to offer me. She does not paint through me, but if I get stuck on how to do something technically, she offers suggestions.

Years later, after traveling to Japan, I received the spiritual gift of being able to see the Universal Language of Light symbols in people's auras. These symbols represent the information they brought into this incarnation with them. Spirit suggested that I start making paintings for people of their symbols and the energies of the Rays that would most support them to accomplish their life's purpose. One day while in the studio, I received a message to do a soul painting with peacock feathers in the background. Fortunately I had one peacock feather to look at. I did the painting, which was very detailed and difficult for me to capture the images of the peacock feathers. The painting had not been ordered by anyone, but when I completed it Spirit asked that I call a meditation teacher I had met previously in Littleton, CO. I called and explained the painting to this woman and the circumstances under which I had received it. I was uncomfortable doing so, since she had not ordered it. I explained what had happened and what the painting looked like. I told her that I would mail it to her, if she was receptive to having it, and that I would not expect her to pay for it since she had not ordered it.

She said she was sure the painting was hers, because she had peacocks on her property. She said she would feel better giving me something energetically in exchange for the painting. I felt compelled to ask her if she knew where I could obtain a set of what I had heard referred to as the *I AM Discourses* or the "green books" channeled by the Ascended Masters to Mr. and Mrs. Guy Ballard in the early 1930's. She began to laugh. "The books are available from my website which is called Peacock Publishing," she said. "I will send you the whole set of thirteen books. It will be the perfect barter for the painting."

I've had the tapes of the material I channeled from Saint Germain since 1990 and I've had the *I AM Discourses* books since 1992, but I've never taken time to read them all or to transcribe the channeled tapes. A few weeks ago, it was suggested by Saint Germain that it is time to get the I AM information out to people in a condensed and updated format. During these weeks that I'm undergoing chemo and radiation, I will focus on doing the transcription and gleaning from the tapes and the *I AM Discourses* books what the Hierarchy wants to say at this time about consciously interacting with our I AM Presence, what they call the "new spiritual technology." I apparently agreed in my soul contract to perform this service.

If you wish to have the *I AM Discourses* books yourself, as well as the condensed version you will be receiving, you may order them from the Peacock Publishing website or from the Saint Germain Press, Inc., 1120 Stonehedge Dr., Schaumburge, IL60194, 708-882-1911. They are also available from Amazon. I am sure if you Google "I AM Presence" it will take you to their website.

I had the cancer removed and I did chemotherapy and radiation in order to keep it from reoccurring in another part of my body.

I agreed to have this dis-ease in order to put in Human consciousness a matrix of "healing cancer without fear." It has been proven that when one person accomplishes something, such as running the three minute mile, swimming the English Channel or any other seemingly unattainable feat, that matrix is then in Human consciousness and, thereafter, anyone who chooses to discipline themselves to do so could accomplish the task.

2.

Finding the I Am Presence

Until 1982, a perfectionist lived in me who believed one won love and approval by doing. I defined myself by the roles I played for others and the lists and agendas that made up my life. I believed we are valued for what we do, not for who we are. I continually accepted one more job and one more job at the church. I knew this was pleasing to others and I hoped it would be pleasing to God. In my confusion of what God really expects of us, and what I thought would please other people, I took four Valium a day in order to appear to be in control of my life and my emotions.

In my case, it took losing everything I cherished to find I could not climb the ladder of doingness to reach God, but had to stop completely and go within myself and get still and quiet enough to hear my own inner God voice. After every role I thought was me was removed, I sat with a legal pad on my lap and wrote I am... I am... and tried to figure out what I was now that I wasn't a banker, wife, mother, daughter, sister, lover, Episcopalian, secretary or president of this and that. At that point, I had no idea I was giving myself the real answer of who I am with all my roles removed. I AM the vehicle through which the I AM can express itself in Human form. Fortunately, it does not take losing everything, or even deliberately giving up everything as monks do, to reach a conscious awareness of God. It takes silence. God is always there, has always been there, waiting to be recognized and to listen within us.

In the solitude and silence, I first had to face my anger, hurt, greed, self-absorption, envy, apathy, hatred, bitterness, cynicism and grief before I could be ready to hear anything God had to say to me. I was really pissed at God and myself for getting me into such a painful place in my life. At first, the pain of loss seemed larger than I was. It took three years of looking inside myself and sorting these unresolved feelings before I could clear enough space to see the light within. I had to sort them and give them up, see that they were not real. They were just my reaction to the events. They were not who I AM.

I AM now sustained by the belief that God is available at any moment, that no matter how deep, shallow or seemingly trivial my need is; I am never beyond divine guidance. I had to reach a point where I was willing to get the lesson and not hold on to the pain of the event.

I'm often reminded of those Russian Matrioshka dolls where there is a doll inside a doll and another doll inside of that doll and on and on. I often use this image when trying to explain the over lighting of our Oversoul, but I also think of it as all the "me's" inside of me. I think of it as all the levels of my Oversoul that I can access telepathically if I'm not too scared to allow it. It also can represent the Human family, or all of creation. Each party is unique and independent, but nevertheless inextricably linked and belonging to the larger whole. We contain the others and we are ourselves contained by God.

I met a psychotherapist once, not in a professional setting but when she attended a lecture I gave, and she accused me of being stuck in my story. "Why do you start your teaching by telling and retelling your story? Your story isn't important. What you've learned from it is all that is important." I explained that if I only shared what I believed I had learned, without sharing the story of the struggle of how I got there, it would not make it possible for people to relate or use the information. She wrote me a long letter and explained that she no longer wanted to have anything to do with me and that she wanted me to stay away from her clients and not to counsel or read for any of them anymore. I ignored her suggestion and continued to share my story and what I had learned.

Years later she sent another letter of apology, saying she had learned that sharing our stories and what we've learned from our experiences is all we actually have to share with anyone. She now has a profession of making scrapbooks and written history of other people's lives to give to their families.

In the beginning years of telling my story over and over, I would each time relive the pain of abandonment of my Mother's death, my father re-marrying so soon to someone no one knew (including him), my divorce, my fiancé's death, being excommunicated from the Episcopal Church, letting my children live with their father in another state and my attempt to end my life by jumping off a sailboat in the middle of the Pacific to kill myself.

Then, one day my soul found a funny way to tell the story and I found myself laughing with my soul as I told the story. That day there were tears in the eyes of those who had had similar feelings and experiences. But they were also able to laugh with me at the humor of how tragic events, when looked at in retrospect, Sometimes shows how the soul was changing our path, giving us one more opportunity to be real, to be whole, to wake up to the truth of who we are. At the time we are in the middle of the change, it can feel painful and awful and make us really sad and angry, but once we've lived through it, hopefully, we can see the soul's motive and appreciate that it might have taken something horrific to get us out of our rut, our pseudo-security. Perhaps we can also stop beating ourselves up for making rash or wrong decisions.

> *"The shortest distance between a Human being*
> *and Truth is a story."*
> **– Anthony de Mello**

As long as we are still using as our identity that I am a doctor, lawyer, housewife, secretary, real estate salesperson, artist, musician, wife, mother, husband, etc., rather than I AM, the I AM of God which is causing my heart to beat, a conduit through which God is expressing itself as a writer, waiter, salesperson, massage therapist, etc., we will be living from a place that is not truly who we are.

In writing or telling our story, we want to make sure we look for and point out the places or connections where we were drawn into a situation to learn a lesson from God. The struggles can lead us to the true meaning of life, our true identity and the truth, if we are paying attention. If we are busy blaming God or someone else, we won't get the lesson and we will need another experience. I believe "attention" is the one thing God expects of us, to remain conscious. I believe when we are asked to do something, the most useful thing to ask ourselves, to ask of our souls is: "Is this mine to do?" If we take on things that really were not meant for us, the result will be costly either emotionally, physically or financially.

I've been reading Eckhart Tolle's books *THE POWER OF NOW* and *A NEW EARTH - AWAKENING TO YOUR LIFE'S PURPOSE* and Sue Monk Kidd's FIRSTLIGHT. All of these writings stress how important it is to stay in the present moment. Kidd suggests that "the words *now, here* and *nowhere* have the same arrangements of letters, but differ when a small space is inserted. Likewise, a fine space separates us from experiencing our life as nowhere or now here. Attentiveness is entering fully the moment you are currently in, no matter how hassling or mundane, and simply being totally present with it. It is so easy to get caught up in moving through life on automatic pilot, half-seeing, half-here, our attention abducted by the dreaded small stuff."

It is so easy to lose touch with the inner life of the soul. There is such a profusion of demands and life is now so complex, so many to-do lists, not to mention the inner compulsion to accomplish something. In studying symbols, I was struck by the symbol in the Chinese language for "busyness" which means "heart killing." We must all seek out spots of time that nourish and repair our souls. Spots of time when we stop and just "be."

Begin to observe yourself in the presence of others, friends and strangers, and check your availability. Are you completely present or are you thinking about what you will do or say next? Are you judging them as you watch or paying attention to the God within them? Are you being mindfully available? We are invited by God to just "be" with people, not to fix, cure or solve their problems, but to just "be" present. When we are with others with the intention of listening to fix or solve their problems, we take our energy to the level of theirs and the level of the energy of the problem. If we just stay "present" with our "Presence", we bring the level of the situation up energetically and often they can then actually "see or hear" what is real or what is really going on in their lives or what is actually called for in the situation. We are not here to fix people. We are here to allow the soul to "be" through us.

Kidd points out that God always works through "process." First there is a seed, then a sprout, then a blossom and finally fruit. God does not begin with the butterfly, but with a larva that becomes a chrysalis and finally a creature with wings. Perhaps most mysterious of all is the unfolding process of ovum, fetus, baby, child, adolescent, adult. The universe is designed to move stage by stage, from incompletion to completion, and so are we. We are each pregnant with Divinity.

We can read something or hear a moving sermon or lecture and decide—from now on I am going to always be a compassionate and loving person. But Kidd says, "You can't force the heart. How often have we set out to love the World—or even more difficult, to love some tiresome, undeserving, mule-headed person on our street—and given up, feeling exasperated, unappreciated, used, tired, burned out, or just plain cynical? The point is, you don't arbitrarily make up your mind to be compassionate so much as you choose to follow a journey that transforms your heart into a compassionate space."

In the South, we have a tendency to speak our minds, but we are also taught manners. We might say he is the most tactless, meanest, most boring person I've ever met, bless his heart. Tacking on the "bless his heart" somehow softens and actually does bless the person for whom, at that moment, we are having difficulty feeling compassion.

I've noticed the same thing happens when I'm unconscious enough to pray for patience, something I often lack. God will send me a myriad of ways to let me test whether or not I can be patient. God doesn't always answer prayer as we expect. Sometimes when we pray for a certain virtue—like patience—God does not necessarily send it to us in a package ready for instant use. We are much more likely to be put in a situation where we are given the opportunity to *develop* that virtue. I've learned it is much wiser to pray for grace and to be grateful for what I have than to pray for patience.

The most significant gifts are often the ones we most easily overlook; small, everyday blessings such as hot and cold running water, health, music, flowers, woods, friends, books, family, fingerprints, photos, fire-places, air conditioning, shoes, appliances that work for us, electronics (when they work) and second chances.

It is easy for me to think what I'm doing is so important I can't stop doing it. We can think we can't slow down because so much is expected of us. We can be irritated by a goose or a turtle crossing the road; or we can stop and watch and appreciate the sun, the trees, and the water and, at this time of year in Oklahoma, the beautiful redbud trees blooming. Wherever we are and whatever is happening, we can always be thinking—we should be somewhere else doing something else or that something other than what is should be happening.

A couple of years ago, Spirit insisted that I needed to be aboard a cruise ship that was going to cruise the Mexican Caribbean. Of course I resisted, because it was ridiculously expensive and Spirit was clear I needed to do this alone. I was allowed by my soul to attend only two of the Abraham lectures during the cruise for which I had paid an extra $400, but from one of the ladies who was at the table where I had dinner every evening I learned a lesson that has served me well. Her favorite saying was, "It is what it is. Now when I think something should be different than it appears to be I can remind myself, "it is what it is" and I have a choice to accept it or change it, but resisting it is futile. Being angry about it is futile. Believing it "should" be some other way doesn't serve me and can make me miserable.

There are miracles to be found in acceptance, which is why the following prayer serves so many so well:

"God, grant me the serenity to accept the things
I cannot change, the courage to change the things I can,
and the wisdom to know the difference."
– Reinhold Niebuhr

When I first started doing watercolor, I had trouble waiting for one layer of paint to dry before I added the next, and my paintings would come out looking muddy. It took years for me to develop enough patience to let one layer dry completely before I added another. Actually, I must admit I didn't really learn it in terms of sitting there patiently waiting for it to dry; I just learned to work on four canvases at a time so three were always drying while I worked on the one that was dry. I think in some ways learning to work with our souls instead of going off on tangents works the same way. Learning to use what we've learned thus far leads us to the next layer of learning. If we try to use many different methods of meditating and processing, we will only get muddy on the inside and not like our results. If we simplify our method of opening ourselves to our soul and expecting a response, things become clearer and we find we are much more than we thought. We find that there are layers and layers and layers of "us" within our Oversouls from whom we can receive guidance and assistance.

I never really imagined I could become an artist when it was first suggested to me by my soul. I believe we have no idea how much hidden potential is within us. I read an interesting story in Thoreau's *WALDEN*:

"There was a table made of apple wood, which stood in a farmer's kitchen in New England for sixty years. One day a gnawing sound began to emanate from the table. It kept up for several weeks, until at last a bug emerged from the table, unfurled its wings and took flight. An insect egg had been deposited in the trunk of the apple tree before it was made into a table and had remained in the wood all those years. Warmed, perhaps by the heat of the coffee urn placed on the table, it hatched, and the little bug gnawed its way out."

Who knows what unhatched potential—what dormant seeds—lie in our lives? We are seeded with hidden promise.

When these lives are over, we will not be asked by our souls why we weren't like Jesus, Mother Teresa, Michael Jackson, Monet or Buckminster Fuller, but we will be asked, "Did you use all the gifts you were given? Were you the best you that you could be?"

It is fairly easy to meditate when things around us are quiet, we are in church or we have the perfect meditation music, but I think we are called to remember who we <u>really</u> are in the midst of the noise, the bulk mail, the news, the chaos, the traffic, the emergency room, when someone we love dies, when the doctor gives us a diagnosis we don't expect. If we remember the reason we are in the emergency room, or hooked up to a chemo IV, or under the radiation device, to consciously be a conduit for God's energy, then we can be there in a useful way. We can be there without fear, because we understand we are not the body. We are that which inhabits the body.

Recently I've been doing dot-to-dot pictures with my grandson and it occurred to me that my life is like that. I very often don't know where my life is going or what I'm going to do with the rest of my life, but I have learned that all I really need to know is where the next dot is. It comforts me to know, when I can't see the whole picture in that moment, that all I really need to see is the next dot. There is a divine wisdom in us that simply knows. A nudge, an awareness, a dream, an intuitive flash, a gradual dawning, a gut reaction—guidance comes from within, step by tiny step.

Kidd says: "There is an extraordinary need in our lives for silence. The constant noise and chatter, internal and external, causes us to lose touch with the center of our being. When that happens, we become caught in all kinds of unimportant things. We suffer from this noise. Many of us even cling to this pollution of noise because it drowns our painful hungers or memories inside us. There is an old contemplative saying: 'If you cannot improve the silence, do not speak.'"

Everything is in God and God is in everything.

I highly recommend all of Sue Monk Kidd's books to you. She wrote *The Secret Life of Bees* and *The Mermaid Chair*. Firstlight is a compilation of her early writings. She evolved from organized religion to spirituality, as have many of us.

I also recommend the writings and now teachings on the internet of Eckhart Tolle.

In the meantime, be as much in the present moment as you can. It is not an easy assignment, but one that causes much anxiety to dissolve. Worry and anxiety sap our energy and create nothing.

3.

The I Am Presence
and Saint Germain

Saint Germain is one of the Ascended Masters who has worked tirelessly to assist Earth and Humanity with their evolution. Saint Germain is the Master of the Seventh Ray – the Violet Ray of Transmutation. He had many incarnations on Earth. He has loved Humankind for thousands of years. He worked at the Court of France previous to and during the French Revolution. He is thoroughly linked with America in the past, present and future. He was instrumental in the writing of the Declaration of Independence. He sees America as the vehicle through which enormous amounts of Light can come to Earth and have positive influence on other countries and cultures. He focuses tremendous effort into the protection of freedom for America and the people of America. He gave guidance to President Washington and President Lincoln as they were being instrumental in massive changes in America. He has continually poured his great love into America and the World. He speaks of America as the "Cup of Light" through which Light will pour out around the World. He speaks of the Freedom of America being an example for the World to follow, "so goes America, so goes the World." The current condition of American consciousness and current American politics makes this a somewhat scary thought.

Through the years the Master Saint Germain has given information about the Violet Flame, the Ascended Masters and the I AM PRESENCE to various channels. Through the ages he channeled to Madame Blavatsky in the 1800's and Alice Bailey in the early 1900's. In the 1930-1940's he appeared to a group seeking contact with the Masters at Mt. Shasta, California. They made contact with the Brotherhood of Mt. Shasta, which is a part of the

Great White Brotherhood and the Masters channeled their teachings to Guy Ballard and a group who traveled around America and broadcast the channeled material on the radio to encourage people to form groups to do decrees to attempt to keep the Second World War from moving onto American soil. In the '70's and '80's he channeled to Elizabeth Clare Prophet to create the Summit Lighthouse University. She published many books of his teachings and the teachings of other Ascended Masters. He began to speak to me consistently in 1990-1991 while I was living in Mt. Shasta.

Saint Germain's teaching advocates that each individual set a goal to become a Master and to deliberately raise their vibration and thought toward ultimate ascension at the time of physical death. He advocates that each person use the authority of their own life to command the Light to take dominion on the Earth; to see themselves as Masters.

He says that when an individual makes a conscious effort to correct their weaknesses of thought and habit and seeks the connection with the Ascended Masters; the connection will happen. The Ascended Master Retreat is in and over the Grand Teton in Wyoming. He says of the Ascended Masters: "The more Humanity accepts the presence of Ascended Masters, the wider it opens the door of possibility for our assistance to them. The rejection of the idea of the Ascended Masters does nothing to remove them or to change their influence in the Universe."

When I "channel" information, the information comes into my consciousness in blocks of pure non-verbal thoughts. The rhythm of the downloading of the information does have a suggestion of syntax and vocabulary. I don't always feel comfortable with the vocabulary and syntax. Much of it feels archaic to today's speech and when previously given contains many unnecessary words. When it was channeled, spoken to groups and written previously the purpose of all the additional words was to keep the attention of the audience or the reader for longer periods of time to give more time for them to be exposed to the energy of the Masters. Humanity has evolved and is now ready to experience the information in a shorter form and to receive larger doses of energy within shorter periods of time without damaging their physiology or their emotional bodies.

I have negotiated with Saint Germain and the Spiritual Hierarchy, in certain instances, to change some of the vocabulary and syntax of the channeled material. I do not feel that this compromises the energy of the information, but overall makes it more user friendly. An example of this is that Saint Germain refers to the I AM Presence as your "Mighty I AM Presence." I feel my I AM Presence knows it is "mighty." I feel more comfortable referring to it as "Beloved I AM Presence" or simply as the "I AM Presence." You, of course, should feel free to use the terminology that feels comfortable to you. I feel the same way about the language of the *Bible* and the information I have channeled from the Master Jesus. The following being an example:

God made a covenant with Humanity: *"I will put My Law in their inward parts, and write in their hearts; and will be their God, and they shall be my people...for they shall all know Me, from the least of them unto the greatest of them; for I will forgive their iniquity, and I will remember their sin no more."*

Sometimes during relating this teaching or information to you I will use quotes from the *Bible* simply to point out that this is not new information. We have had it for years, but I don't think (partially because of the vocabulary) that we have totally understood how to work with the information or to work directly with our I AM Presence. According to the Spiritual Hierarchy, it is now time for Humanity to receive this information in an easier to understand format. That is my goal.

THE WORD was in the beginning, and that very word was with God, and God was the Word. St. John 1:1

Was THE WORD "OM, AH AUM, or I AM?"

The Master Jesus is quoted as having said, *"I AM the way, and the truth, and the life."* (John 14:6)

God said, *"Let there be Light,"* and there was Light. He expanded the Light by giving birth to individual Spirit-sparks. These drops of His Cosmic substance were scattered though out the universes as billions of seeds of Light. Each seed has a unique destiny and each seed is fed by the energy of God through its individualized I AM Presence. Each soul spark is created to express an aspect of the individuality of God.

Webster in his definition of Spirit says: "In the abstract, life or consciousness viewed as an independent type of existence. One manifestation of the divine nature is the Holy Spirit."

H. Emilie Cady says in *Lessons of Truth,* "There is but one Source of being. This Source is the living fountain of all good, be it life, love, wisdom, power – the Giver of all good gifts. This Source and you are connected, every moment of your existence. You have the power to draw on this Source for all of the good you are, or ever will be, capable of desiring."

She continues by saying, "If you keep your thoughts turned toward the external of yourself, or of others, you will see only the things that are not real, but temporal, and which pass away. All the faults, failures, or lacks in people or circumstance will seem very real to you, and you will be unhappy and sick. If you turn your thoughts away from the external toward the spiritual, and let them dwell on the good in yourself and in others, all the apparent evil will first drop out of your thoughts and then out of your life."

We can all learn to turn the conscious mind toward Universal Mind, or Spirit within us. We can imagine a great reservoir, out of which lead innumerable rivers or channels. At its farther end, each channel opens out into a small fountain. This fountain is being continually replenished from the reservoir and is itself a radiating center that gives out in all directions that which it receives, so that all who come within its radius are blessed. This is our relation to God. Each one of us is a radiating center. Each of us, no matter how insignificant we may feel in the World, may receive from God unlimited good of whatever kind we desire, and radiate it to all about us. We must radiate it if we are to receive more. If we do not radiate, we become stagnant.

The *Bible* states it this way: "*I AM the vine, ye are the branches; He that abides (consciously) in me, and I in him (in his consciousness), the same beareth much fruit; for apart from me (or severed from me in your consciousness) ye can do nothing...If ye abide in me, and my words abide in you, ask whatsoever ye will, and it shall be done unto you*" (John 15:5,7).

God is All-Good – always good, always love. God never changes, no matter what we do or may have done. God is always trying to pour more of itself through us into visibility to make us larger, fuller, freer individuals. The clearer we are emotionally the more good can come through us.

The energetic connection between Source and the individualized aspects is in the physical heart of the Human. This connection is anchored in a threefold flame representing the trinity of Love, Power and Wisdom. The flames are pink, yellow and blue. The symbol for this trinity is the Fleur de Lis.

I have tremendous gratitude for Shelagh Schopen's work in channeling a visual chart of our connection to our Cosmic Christ Consciousness Self, the Holy Spirit and our I AM Presence. She and Marie Commiskey completed the chart during our stay in Kauai. The chart shows the Violet Flame of Transmutation coming up from below the feet of the individualized person to transmute all obstructions, limitations and negativity. The Fleur de Lis represents the tri-fold flame within the heart. The Holy Spirit is represented by the Dove above the Cosmic Christ image and before the I AM Presence. The image of the Grand Teton, behind the other images connects us energetically with the Ascended Masters Retreat and their energies. You may want to print off a copy of the chart in color and have it laminated to keep near you to remind you of your connection as we proceed with the other lessons about our I AM Presence.

The energy which is causing our hearts to beat is the greatest power in the Universe. It is our I AM Presence. It is the energy of God. At birth only ten percent of our I AM Presence is present in the physical body to keep it alive and to operate all the systems of the body. The remainder of our I AM Presence is above the physical body. God is both within us and above us. We are all a part of God. We could not move or speak were it not for our I AM Presence. At different ages in our lives additional amounts of the I AM Presence energy merges with the physical form. It is my understanding that additional energy is given traditionally, but not always, at the age of six, twelve, sixteen, twenty-one and forty-four. Additional energy can also be given at times of great stress or change in the life of a Human. These times could be referred to as "over lighting" by the I AM Presence. These times are temporary and the energy is only given for stabilization of the life form until the emergency is past.

Our I AM Presence never judges or condemns; it waits until we are spiritually awake enough to recognize its Presence and until we are willing to give obedience to it before it allows larger portions of power to flow through the Human body beyond the forty-forth year. This is why around that age many people have what is thought of as a "mid-life crisis." The additional energy is given to attempt to wake the person from "spiritual amnesia," to awaken a person to the fact that they are not just physical. The energy that makes the difference between whether the doctors pronounce us dead or alive comes from the non-physical dimension. I remember clearly never having had that thought until one night I was in West Texas in a Hugh Prather study group and one of the participants was a heart nurse. She pointed out that the one thing the doctors and scientists had not been able to figure out was where does the energy come from that causes the patient's heart to beat at birth and where does it go when the heart ceases to beat at death?

We are physical counterparts of that which is non-physical and together we are co-creators of Human and Earth reality. The energy coming into the body is pure consciousness until it is qualified by Human feeling and thought. Our feelings and thoughts most often distort the purity of the energy with discord before it acts in the World. Our I AM Presence has the Power and Authority to produce through us everything that we require and desire for ourselves personally, for Humanity and for the Earth, but we must ask and we must have obedience to the suggestions of our I AM Presence.

As Humans we have allowed our intellect to rule. We have believed the appearances of the World more than the energy behind all Creation. Our intellect has led us into a maze of limitations. Conscious connection to our I AM Presence can lead us out of this maze and remove our limitations. Our I AM Presence can offer tremendous clarity to things we are experiencing in our physical dimension. We have a responsibility to acknowledge the God aspect within ourselves and within each individual. Each individualized Presence of God is united with every other individualized Presence of God, with the Heavenly Hosts, and with the whole of Creation. All of Creation is a part of the Creator.

Physical life as we know it could not exist without the existence of the non-physical dimension's energy, support and knowledge. Physical Earth and Humanity are the products of the attention and knowledge of the non-physical dimensions. These larger Beings exist and the only reason we do not see them is because of the difference in the frequency of vibrations. An understanding of the relationship between the physical and non-physical dimensions is essential to a productive and satisfying physical experience. As long as we think of the non-physical realm as big, vague, mysterious, and misunderstood, we will find it impossible to find our purpose and place within the Universe. We won't understand why we exist and we won't understand what we are to do now that we do exist.

Much of our misunderstanding comes from our perceptions about death. There is no death. There is only life experiencing life in different dimensions of vibration. There is a part of us that is here in this dimension and there are parts of us that are in the non-physical dimensions. Some people would refer to these parts as the Oversoul, the Higher Self or simply as the Soul. But for the purpose of this teaching coming from Saint Germain, we shall refer to that part of the self as the Higher Mental Body, which is the same as the Cosmic Christ Consciousness aspect of ourselves, and the I AM Presence that is vibrationally above the Higher Mental Body and between ourselves and the Source of Creation, God. These non-physical counterparts of ourselves are infinitely and intricately aware of us at all times. Because of the Law of Freewill they are not allowed to intervene on our behalf, or on behalf of Humanity or the Earth, unless we ask.

Through each physical incarnation each soul aspect is seeking experience, stimulation and growth. We sometimes wonder why we do not remember having lived before. Many people seek to remember through regression, as I did. Once I accessed the Akashic records it seemed to me to be an inefficient system that wiped the memory slate clean each time and sent us down to begin anew and learn everything all over again every time with no memory. But, eventually, my soul convinced me that it would be harder if we did remember. All those details would cause great confusion. It is not necessary to recall past lives to receive benefit of all that experience. We have never been and we shall never be separated from our I AM PRESENCE, which holds all of that information. Through our connection to our I AM Presence we can have access to all the important conclusions that were drawn from those experiences.

We are constantly creating or miss creating. Through conscious contact with our I AM Presence, we can purify and transmute any misqualified energy or creation. Everyone has the potential to contact their own I AM Presence through intention. Our first step in making this connection is use of the Law of Forgiveness for ourselves and all others. Forgiveness must occur before healing can be accomplished, whether we are talking about an individual, a race, or a country. There are thousands of Ascended Masters and they have used this same method of watching their thoughts, correcting their beliefs, changing their habits, asking for and giving forgiveness to prepare themselves for ascension. The method to ascension is the same for anyone.

When Saint Germain first began to speak to me about the value of decrees, I was resistant. I was a person who had prayed all my life. When I began to expand my consciousness I exposed myself to the idea of mantras, chants, and affirmations, but I didn't really understand why decrees would be more efficient and of course being a practical person interested in efficiency I wanted to know the difference. I had also spent some time studying Science of Mind or Religious Science and been exposed to spiritual mind treatments. I have made an effort to bring you definitions of each in order to put forth an idea of why one might be more effective than another.

DEFINITIONS

PRAYER: a petition, entreaty, supplication, thanksgiving, adoration, or confession to God, a saint or an object of worship. A formula or sequence of words appointed for praying such as the Lord's Prayer.

INVOCATION: the act of invoking or calling upon a deity or Spirit for aid, protection or inspiration; a petition for help or aid from God; a form of prayer invoking God's presence; a call to God, or to beings who have become one with God, to release power, wisdom, and love to Humankind or to intercede on behalf of Humanity; supplication for the flow of Light, energy, peace, and harmony to come into manifestation on Earth as it is in Heaven.

MANTRA: a word or formula of sounds, often in Sanskrit, to be recited or sung for the purpose of intensifying the action of the Spirit of God in Human.

CHANT: a short simple melody used in singing the psalms or canticles in a service. In both the East and West, the name of God is chanted over and over again in the ritual of at-one-ment whereby the soul of the Human becomes one with the Spirit of God by intonation of the sound of the name of God. This is given in Sanskrit as AUM or AUM TAT SAT AUM and in English as I AM THAT, I AM. By sounding the name of God, or that of a member of the Heavenly Hosts, the vibration of the being is simulated and thereby the Being itself is drawn to the one chanting. Therefore chants, when properly used, magnetize the Presence, whether universal or individualized, of the Divine Consciousness.

DECREE: a foreordaining will an edict or fiat, a foreordaining of events. To decree: verb: to decide, to declare, to command or enjoin; to determine or order; to ordain.

The decree is the most powerful of all applications to the Godhead. It is the command of the son or daughter of God made in the name of the I AM PRESENCE and the Christ for the will of the Almighty to come into manifestation as above so below. It is the means whereby the kingdom of God becomes a reality here and now through the power of the spoken Word. It may be short or long and usually marked by a formal preamble and a closing, or acceptance.

FIAT: an authoritative decree, sanction, order; a pronouncement; a short dynamic invocation using the name of God, I AM, as the first word of the fiat, such as, I AM the Way! I AM the Truth! I AM the Resurrection and the Life!

Fiats are always exclamations of Christ-power, Christ-wisdom, and Christ-love consciously affirmed and accepted in the here and now.

AFFIRMATION: assertion that something exists or is true; confirmation or ratification of the truth; solemn declaration.

Affirmations are fiats which may be of greater length or more specific detail. They affirm the action of Truth in the Human – in his being, consciousness, and World. They are used alternately with denials of the reality of evil in all of its forms. They affirm the power of Truth.

THE CALL: (noun) a demand, a claim, a request or command to come or be present; an instance of asking for something; the act of summoning the Lord, or the Lord's summoning of His offspring. (Verb) To speak in a loud or distinct voice so as to be heard at a distance; to recall from death or the astral plane; to utter in a loud or distinct voice; to announce or read loudly or authoritatively.

The call is the most direct means of communication between Humans and God, and God and Humanity, frequently used in an emergency, as in: "God, help me!" or "Archangel Michael, take command."

SPIRITAL MIND TREATMENT: An effective mind treatment is motivated and propelled by a consciousness of love and a realization that the Creative Spirit is always at work. We need not compel the Force to work. It is the nature of Creative Power to take form and it is the nature of Humans to use IT. A spiritual mind treatment should be given in a calm, expectant manner and with a deep inner conviction of its reality, without any fear or any sense that the Human mind must make it effective. The work is effective because the Law is always in operation.

A spiritual mind treatment begins with a declaration of Oneness with the Creative Force of the Universe. This declaration is normally followed by denial of the seeming circumstance of the disturbance or illness. Every objective evidence contrary to good should be denied, and in its place should come a sense of right action and a claiming of unity with the Spirit within all things. This denial should be followed by a declaration of truth about the person, stating that this person is a Divine Being, complete, happy, satisfied, and conscious of their own spiritual being. Declaring that this condition, which is causing the suffering now, is not a law and has no right to be and is no longer effective through this individual. Declare yourself or the person you are treating for as free from it. Ask to remove any obstruction in mind, or any manifested obstruction allowing the flow of life to be resumed unobstructed within the individual. After the denial and declaration a claiming of the situation or person as now free from the condition or obstacle is appropriate. It is also appropriate to claim that the condition can never return. Claim that this is now the truth about the person or situation. When a spiritual mind treatment is offered a definite, conscious idea has been set in motion in the Subjective World, which accepts ideas literally and acts upon them. The results to us may appear to be a miracle, but in actuality it is the working of the Law.

We might begin a mind treatment with the statement: "With God all things are possible, God can find a way." It does not matter so much what one says, it is what one believes when they say it that counts.

A Spiritual Mind Treatment – From: *Change We Must – My Spiritual Journey* by Nana Veary

"I now let God's greatness manifest in me. All power is instantly available at every point in space and every instant of time. I know this, and all fear is erased from my consciousness. I join with all those who know God as the only Power and Presence in their lives. God in me is my resource, and nothing can harm me. I know that I AM the cause of my experiences. Love attends me wherever I go. Peace envelopes me at every moment. The more I know of God, the less I create or experience difficulties. I steadfastly watch my thoughts. I concentrate my consciousness to Truth. The endless possibilities of life are before me, and nothing can prevent my full spiritual development. I know that I AM growing in spiritual and factual demonstrations. I AM the victorious creation of God, and triumph in all my ways. I live with ease, for my thinking is right and my World responds to my decisions. I AM fully conscious that my word eliminates every bondage, whether in myself or others. I claim good judgment. I claim the integrity of God as mine today.

I now accept the creative action of the words I have spoken as Law. They go forth into immediate fulfillment right now. Nothing can prevent them from being fully and completely fulfilled in my experience."

The Master Saint Germain promotes the use of decrees.

4.

Saint Germain's Recommended Decrees and Affirmations

When we do a decree, which is done aloud, or an affirmation, which can be written or read aloud, the most important ingredient is the emotion with which we decree or read aloud the desire. Feeling is the fuel that causes the manifestation or desire to become materialized in this dimension.

It is always important to remember that it is safe to give your life to God. Your life has always been God's. You believing it was your life has always been an illusion. Your heart beats, because of God, your soul chooses to cause it to continue to beat. You are still alive at the discretion of your soul. Your soul has faith that you will wake up and remember this fact. Any information you receive from your soul is merely a suggestion not an order. You always maintain your Freewill, even when you turn the body over to be used by the soul or your I AM Presence. If your soul suggests that you do something that you feel is too challenging or risky it is important to write a list of "conditions under which I could do that are." Write out what you would expect from your soul or the Universe before you could feel comfortable to move in the direction suggested. You were never meant to be a pawn of the soul or your I AM Presence. Your life was always intended to be a cooperative venture between the body, your mind and the soul or your I AM Presence. Co-creation of a joyful, healthy, abundant, stress free life was always the soul's intention when incarnating.

I believe I've read all of what Saint Germain has channeled in our lifetime about spirituality and decreeing. From the reading and what he is suggesting as a way for me to distill down the pertinent information, this is what we've come up with, the importance of the I AM Presence and the importance of decreeing.

I am choosing to use the term "Beloved" instead of "Mighty" in reference to my I AM Presence. This is a personal preference on my part and if it feels more comfortable to use the term "Mighty I AM Presence" feel free to do so.

HEALTH AND HEALING

"I call forth a tube of Master Light from my I AM Presence around my body. I call forth the Violet Consuming Flame to rise up from below my feet to consume all discord, doubt, fear, misqualified energy, anger, disbelief, and disease." I was unaware until recently that the correct way to use the Violet Flame was to call it forth in an upward motion. I had assumed we should call it forth down our own energetic stream from Source as we would to send up a beam of energy to connect to our own Higher Self or Cosmic Christ Consciousness.

"Beloved I AM Presence, Beloved Holy Christ Self, I call forth my I AM Presence to draw to me now the Violet Transmuting Flame about my four lower bodies transmuting all that is less than Christ Perfection."

"God is, and all there is, is God. This Presence and Power are within me, flowing through me as harmony, health, peace, joy, right action, abundance, true expression and inspiration. I AM a clear channel for the Divine."

"There is but one Creator, one Presence, and one Power. This Power is within me as my mind and Spirit. This Presence moves through me as harmony, health and peace. I think, speak and act from that standpoint of Infinite Intelligence. I know that thoughts are things, what I feel I attract, and what I imagine I become. Divine right action governs my life. Divine Law and Order operate in all phases of my life. Divine guidance is mine now. Divine success is mine. Divine prosperity is mine. Divine love and wisdom governs all my transactions and God is guiding me now. God knows the answer."

"I consciously claim the healing love of the Power that created me is dissolving all cells in my body which do not belong. I AM a temple of the living God."

"God is love, and God's love fills my soul and body. God is peace and God's peace fills my mind and body. God is perfect health and God's health is my health. God is joy and God's joy is my joy and I feel wonderful."

"The Infinite Healing Presence is making me whole and perfect."

"Whatever I need to know comes to me from the Cosmic Power within. Infinite Intelligence is operating through me revealing to me what I need to know."

"I AM healthy, happy, successful and prosperous."

"I walk in the Light and all good is mine. The fullness of God is made manifest in all departments of my life. I constantly vision for myself and for others, health, prosperity and all the blessings of life."

"Beloved I AM Presence charge me with your Perfect Health and sustain it, release your Mighty currents of energy into my body now."

"My perfect health is eternally sustained."

"I AM full cosmic obedience to my Beloved I AM Presence and the Ascended Hosts."

"I AM the Cosmic Victory of all the Divine Desires of my being and World in everything I do forever."

"I deliberately call forth the Full Power of my Selective Intelligence and my Power of Discrimination into action from my I AM Presence."

"I call forth the tube of liquid Light from my I AM Presence to surround and protect my body and bring it into perfect balance. I give the use of this body over to my I Am Presence. I ask to have removed all that is not in harmony with my I AM Presence."

"The miraculous healing Cosmic Power is flowing through me now and permeating every atom of my being."

"My heart is a healthy living center working perfectly through which the

Love of God flows to bless me and all others I encounter."

"I AM a birth less, deathless, ageless Spirit."

"I AM a manifestation of God, and every moment God's life, love, wisdom, and power flow into and through me. I AM one with God and I AM governed by God's Law and Love."

"I AM erasing every pattern of disease in my sub-conscious mind and restoring the patterns of perfect health."

"The Cosmic Healing Power which made my body and all its organs knows all the processes and functions of my body, and the miraculous healing Power is permeating every atom of my being, making me whole and perfect. All my organs are God's ideas and through the Power of the Almighty they are functioning perfectly now."

"I give completely into the control of my Higher Mental Body; my I AM Presence, my feelings, my body, my thoughts, and my actions."

"I accept the Invincible Power of Perfection and Protection are permanently sustained within my life and body."

"I call forth to my I AM Presence and my body intelligence to create ample white and red blood cells to keep my body and blood in perfect health and balance."

"I call forth from my I AM Presence the Violet Flame of Transmutation to dissolve all viruses, fungus, misqualified cells and negative energy from within my body and aura."

"I AM perfect health; my sight and hearing are restored to their original perfection."

"I stand in the midst of eternal opportunity, which is forever presenting me with creative ideas and opportunity for expression."

"I accept that which is ready to express through me now."

"I now give full dominion over my body, mind and emotions to my I AM Presence. I call forth my I AM Presence to erase all cause, effect, record and memory of everything which has ever caused disturbance within my physical and emotional bodies."

"I call forth to my I AM Presence for Harmony, Happiness, Health and Strength."

"I AM healthy. My body releases waste products daily, easily and painlessly."

"I allow the Power of my I AM Presence to flood forth without limit to reform my Human form into perfection."

"I AM strong physically, mentally, emotionally and spiritually. I AM pain free."

"I surrender the entire direction of all the Substance of My Being and World to my Beloved I AM Presence and the Ascended Masters Octave of Light and Life."

"I command through my I AM Presence that everything about and around me become the Cosmic Flame of Cosmic Victory of the Cosmic Christ."

"I charge the atmosphere around me with the Cosmic Flame of Cosmic Victory."

"I Command every cell of my body to become the Cosmic Love and Victory of the Cosmic Christ."

"I command every particle of my flesh to rise into the Cosmic Flame of Cosmic Victory and Perfection."

"I AM God operating through my personality for the benefit of Earth, all life on the Earth and beyond."

"I AM God in perfect health."

"I AM God in perfect wisdom."

"I AM God in perfect knowing."

"I AM God in perfect love."

"I AM God in perfect heart."

"I AM God in perfect feelings."

"I AM God in perfect sight."

"I AM God in perfect eyes."

"I AM God in perfect perception."

"I AM God in perfect speech."

"I AM God in perfect hearing."

"I AM God in perfect listening."

"I AM God in perfect elimination of waste products and toxins from my body daily, easily and painlessly."

"Spirit, Divine Life and Energy flow freely to every part of my being, cleansing, revitalizing and restoring me to Perfect Health."

"I now surrender every personal doubt, fear or hard feeling that might retard the perfect flow of life through me. There is no obstruction, no barrier in my mind, my veins or my affairs. I AM harmonious, peaceful, free and unafraid."

"The Laws of Harmony, Grace and Beauty are now governing my life."

"I call forth the Healing Flame of Victory to heal all of my body. I AM Perfect Health eternally sustained."

"I AM filled with peace, strength, power and decision of Spirit. The life forces flow freely, peacefully and harmoniously through every atom of my body. I AM perfect now. My body is pure spiritual substance and as such it is perfect and harmonious."

"By day and by night I AM seeing more and more of God's love, Light, truth and beauty in every person and in everything. God within is healing me now and I give thanks for my perfect health, vision and hearing."

"The Infinite Presence which created me governs my mind and body and is healing me now. My I AM Presence is now transforming, healing, and restoring every cell of my body to perfection."

"Beloved I AM Presence, take command of my body and mind; produce your Perfection and hold your Dominion. Pour your Mighty Light through this body, out into my World and activity, fill it with your Harmony, Your Directing Intelligence and hold it there forever."

"Beloved I AM Presence I accept your full perfection in my mind, body, my World of action. Therefore, charge it with your perfection, your purity and your consuming power of action that dissolves and consumes every discordant thing that has ever been drawn about me."

Say to any disturbing influence or circumstance: "You have no power so far as my world is concerned."

"Beloved I AM Presence take command of my mind and body as yours; produce your perfection by your Dominion. Release your currents of energy into my body and world to cleanse and purify it. Sweep out of my path every obstacle and any destructive thing. Replace it with your Light. Let your Light hold Dominion before me. I ask to be charged with Self-Luminous, Intelligent Substance of Light."

"I call forth the Great Central Sun's Sacred Fire Love to bless this home."

"I call forth from my I AM Presence a tube of Light to keep away from me the pressure of the outer World's discord and the imperfections that have been generated by Humankind."

FOR EARTH AND HUMANITY

"I give my body, mind and emotions over to my I AM Presence to be used for the good of my soul, the Earth and Humanity."

"I call forth the Sacred Fire's Purifying Love to cover all of Earth and all beings living on Earth."

"I call forth the Sacred Fire's Illuminating Love into every bit of Substance, Energy and Consciousness in this World."

"I call forth the Ascended Masters' Sacred Cosmic Fire Love into this World to consume all that is vibrationally less than that love."

"I call forth the Ascended Masters' Sacred Fire Love Eternal Security around me and everything in my World."

"I AM an Open Door through which the Sacred Fire comes to Earth."

"I allow the divine resonance of God to pour through me to touch everything within my sphere of influence."

"There is perfect and divine order in every organ and function of my body. Spirit flows through me and is never obstructed by anything unlike Itself."

"Every idea of my body is now complete and perfect and functions according to Divine Law."

"Everything I eat is perfectly assimilated and serves to raise the vibration of my body. All that is not needed is easily eliminated by my body."

MANIFESTATION

"I am the Victory of this which I desire..."

"I AM a clear, open channel of the Divine. Infinite Life flows unobstructed through me as healing, peace, prosperity and right action. I AM constantly receiving creative ideas."

"I AM led, guided and inspired by the Living Spirit of Love and of Right Action. I AM compelled to move in the right direction and to always know what to do, where and how to do it."

"I have absolute faith in God and all things good. I AM one with the Cosmic Power, and to be one with God is a majority. I know that God and the Universe are for me, and nothing is against me. I AM absolutely fearless, as I know the thing I might fear does not exist – it has no power; it is only a shadow in my mind, and a shadow has no power. I AM full of faith and con-fidence. I have the courage to meet all problems head on, and I overcome them through the wisdom and power of God within me. God's power is with my thoughts of good. I AM immersed in the Divine Presence. God's love fills my soul, and His River of peace flows through me. There is no fear in love, for love and recognition of the One Power casts out all fear. Every moment of my life I AM growing in faith, courage, and confidence and I feel the power of the Almighty flowing through me now. I AM at peace."

"I know there is only One Mind that created all things, and my mind is one with that Mind. I meditate on my inseparable oneness with this Cosmic Mind Power and without strain or stress or any great mental effort, I let my thoughts and mental images sink into my deeper Mind; I AM quiet in the assurance that these thoughts will return, fabricated and manifested by Cosmic Mind who created the Universe."

"I know God is the Cosmic Mind Power, which is the reality of me. My work is God's work, for God works through me and my work cannot be hindered or delayed. The Cosmic Mind Power that created all things finished whatever it created. My work goes through to completion in Divine Order. All that I set out to do reaches fruition. I entertain only those thoughts that make for my highest happiness, peace of mind and achievement."

"I AM grateful to now know and understand all messages coming to me from my soul."

"I AM the Resurrection and the Life of My Divine Plan, physically manifest here and now."

FINANCE & DEBT

"I AM totally debt free through financial abundance. My wallet is always filled with cash and my mailbox is filled with negotiable checks made payable to me. I pay all of my financial obligations before they are due. I AM in a state of financial freedom."

"I AM God in perfect financial abundance."

"I now accept Financial Freedom eternally sustained in my life."

"I call forth to my I AM Presence to release from Its Treasure House an unlimited supply of money and all I need and desire to fulfill my mission. I now accept financial freedom."

"God's wealth is now circulating through me in my World."

"I now claim my portion of the wealth of the Knights Templar in my physical World."

"I choose absolute abundance and perfect health. I know there is no limit in the Universe, the limitation is only in my mind and emotions and I release these limitations now. I see total abundance for everyone on Earth."

"There is a continuous movement of supply towards me, of money and all that I need and desire to express my fullest life."

"Everything necessary to my full and complete expression and experience of joy is mine now."

GOD IS THE SOURCE OF MY SUPPLY.

"In this moment my good comes to me, enough to spare, give and share. My good can never be exhausted or depleted, because the Source from which my good comes is inexhaustible."

"All of my credit card balances are paid in full. I pay the balances completely at the end of each billing cycle."

"I AM the boundless wealth of the Universe in expression."

"I AM free to be myself and free to follow Spirit's suggestions with abundance to spare."

"I AM financially and physically free to go and do all that my soul suggests. I choose total freedom, perfect health and lavish wealth."

"I AM successful in all I do and I AM compensated well for all my efforts."

"I AM the Spirit of Infinite Plenty individualized. I AM boundless abundance in radiant expression. What is expressed in love must be returned in full measure. Therefore wave after wave of visible money supply flows to me now. I AM a money magnet and oceans of money flow to me now. I AM wonderfully rich in consciousness. I AM bountifully supplied with money. I now realize my plan for abundant living. I see my bank account and wallet continually filled with all sufficiency to meet every need with surplus. I lovingly see myself sharing this bounty for the good of all according to Spirit's guidance. I happily see every bill paid in full now. I joyfully see the continuing flow of money that comes to me used with love and wisdom to the highest good of all."

5.

Violet Flame of Transmutation and Freedom
What Is It and How to Use It

CHANNELED FROM SAINT GERMAIN TO bj King

Earth is moving from the Age of Pisces into the Age of Aquarius as of January 18, 2016. Dispensations are being given that will not come about again for another 25,000 years. One of the gifts being offered to us by God at this time is the Violet Flame of Transformation and Freedom from the Seventh Ray Master Saint Germain. He is personally offering this gift for our personal use for clearing the astral realm of negative thought forms and lost souls. It can be used to clear our Human consciousness, the atmosphere of Earth and our four lower bodies. The Violet Fire Ray has a synthesizing effect upon Humanity. It is of a very high vibration and its activity is raising the level of vibrations of all those upon the face of the Earth. It can eliminate the veils, obstructions and hindrances which are preventing closer contact with our Christ Self and I Am Presence.

The administering of the Violet Flame and its use is done through intention. Everything happens because of intention. This Flame can be called forth and used by each and every individual upon the Earth. We may use it to clear our four lower bodies. To do this, we must use it deliberately, persistently and consistently, even many times a day, because we are working to remove debris of many, many lifetimes. We may call for the Violet Fire to transmute situations which are effects of causes past. We can also call it forth to prevent situations from occurring, which we see building before us. We may use it to transmute anything in our lives that is less than our own True Christ Perfection.

We can picture ourselves within a tube of pure White Christ Light. (I envision a tube of light like we used to see aboard Starship Enterprise on Star Trek.) This Christ Light emanates from our I Am Presence and is always with us, but it is up to us to expand it by intention from a pilot light to a massive searchlight. Within this tube of Christ Light, we can add the Violet Flame Light swirling within the tube with us as it burns away all of the dross and dense material we have accumulated over many lifetimes. We can call specifically for it to blaze and transmute all Human negative feelings and desires from our being and all mis-qualified energy for which we are responsible. We can intend the Violet Fire to swirl around us blazing and burning away this density.

Saint Germain suggests we learn and use the following decree:
Beloved Mighty I AM Presence,
Beloved Holy Christ Self,
I am drawing to me now the
Violet Transmuting Flame,
Blazing in, through and
About my four lower bodies,
Transmuting all that is
Less than Christ Perfection.

If you feel unworthy, use this decree: "Blaze away from me, Violet Fire, all unworthiness, that I may see the Perfection that I Am." With these simple words, heartfelt and mind controlled, we are invincible and have the power of the Mighty I Am Presence.

If you cannot visualize the Violet Fire, get something that is of violet hue such as a piece of cloth, a picture of an amethyst. Visualize and energize your thoughts and transmute your life into Christ Perfection. Over stim-ulation is not possible with the use of the Violet Fire and it cannot be exhausted.

It is suggested that we make this a daily ritual to blaze Violet Fire all around us, our World and all with whom we come into contact. Doing this, we can transmute our desires into aspiration, our thoughts into true perception and our knowledge into wisdom. It is especially recommended that we do this ritual upon arising and just before going to bed: when we do it just before going to bed, our soul will work through the night to clear us even more.

It is useful also for us to intend the Blue flame of Power, God's Will and Illumination within our forehead. This unites the Threefold Flame in our hearts and brings us into Oneness with the Pure White Light of the Source of all Creation. We are beings of Fire and Divine energies and we have the power to increase our frequency through intention, breath and meditation.

It is our duty to learn the manipulation of the Rays of Divine Energy coming from the Heart of God which are being given to us for our conscious knowledge and use. The achieving of Divinity, the manifest action of the Will of God, is the purpose; participating in the Divine Plan for Humankind is the objective. Each person in their own right is a Divine Being and our part in the Plan is to aid the development of those of lesser Light. There is a balance which must be achieved on Earth between each and every individual within themselves and then with their group. The Divine Directive is that we all come to remember and accept that we are the children of God and are made in the image and likeness of God to be co-creators with God.

The Seventh Ray, the Ray of Ceremonial Magic, Transmutation and Freedom, is God's gift to us. Through the use of this energy we can wield this Mighty Power and become agents within the Spiritual Hierarchy implementing the Divine Plan of God for Earth, Humanity and all life on Earth. It is the most beneficial gift Humankind has ever been given by God. We have an obligation to use it and direct it for transmuting negative thoughts and also for increasing the Cosmic Christ Consciousness within Humankind.

We are asked to call it forth to erase all errors and break down all barriers between people and nations and to burn away glamour and illusions that are inhibiting Humans from remembering their true identity. It is important for us to engulf the Earth and Humanity in this permeating atmosphere of Love, Transmutation and Freedom.

If we look at the World through rose colored glasses of Love and turn our eyes skyward, the Love energy blends with the blue of the sky and becomes violet. Feel this energy permeating you, every cell and atom of your being vibrating, energizing you, revitalizing you and radiating from you. See that you are a bearer of Light and Love and that you carry this forward with conscious direction to those areas in which you travel, knowing that you are aiding the cause and furthering the Divine Plan of God.

We are to think violet always, it is warming or cooling. It transmutes any situation in which we find ourselves. It is the Synthesizing Ray for this Age and makes all things whole. We are all warriors in the intention for Light to dominate the Planet and its population with Christ Light.

If we hold or wear an amethyst, we shall direct, consciously and visibly, the Violet Fire with special blessings. We have the responsibility to consciously wield and direct, to consciously transmute, and to consciously realize the effects of that which we do. It is the Will of God to which we all attain, and through this Will the effects of the Violet Flame are seen.

Saint Germain and the Angel Zadkiel, who is the Archangel of the Seventh Ray, warn that to attempt to use this power for personal ends or selfish gains will have a boomerang effect upon us. But if we let our souls guide us, it will shine through and direct us always.

The Violet Flame is very powerful, but it is not instantaneous; consistent usage is required to produce results. The results are gradual and ongoing. We must be persistent. That which has taken a long time to accumulate will take a while to clear and disintegrate.

Energy follows thought and Saint Germain has assured us that if we are persistent in our use of the Violet Flame, we will see results in ourselves as well as in the clearing of the effluvia around the Earth.

We are needed at this time to become members of the Spiritual Hierarchy in manifestation. To qualify for this service, it is required that we clear our four lower bodies and connect directly in consciousness with our souls. We must be clear enough to respond to the intuitive impulses from our soul with clear perception. Our limitations can be cleared through the use of the Violet Flame. The work we do for the benefit of all Humankind is bringing in the Golden Age, the Age of Aquarius.

We can use this power without fear because no harm can come to us or others by our use of the Flame and it cannot be over used. There is no limitation on it other than what we might put upon ourselves. If we use it every minute, every hour, we will feel it working because we will have an increased sense of freedom. We can demand and command it. It is ours for the asking.

If ascension is our choice to not need to reincarnate, we can use the Flame continually. We can see ourselves enclosed in the Violet Flame and live and move and have our being within it. We can transmute all negativity that comes to us. This form of Divine Alchemy can change emotions into higher qualities. We can use it simply to transmute daily worries into confidence and trust.

We are the Christ Self in action, in physical form upon the Earth. In coming to this realization within our conscious minds, we will dispel all that is less than Christ Perfection.

Conscious attention to detail, constant effort and unrelenting use of the Violet Flame will remove the restrictions we have created through our minds and emotions. Use of the Flame can cause us to feel peaceful when we remember to use it.

Transmute! Transmute! Transmute! Through the use of the Violet Flame any situation you hear of on the planet that is less than perfection.

We are called by the Hierarchy to unify our efforts in groups of Light Workers calling forth the Flame for clearing ourselves and Earth. There is great power multiplied exponentially and intensified when we work in groups. Twelve in a group would give out 12x12=144 units of energy

"One proclaiming his brand of Truth to the exclusion of all others does not change the Truth nor the facts of the matter."
– Saint Germain

It is important for us to develop discernment (pray and ask for the spiritual gift of discernment). It will be our greatest ally in deciding what the Truth is when we are faced with new information, when reading books or listening to lectures.

Saint Germain says we are architects of the Golden Age and that there are many new principles relating to the life of Spirit which must be incorporated into the lifestyle of all Humanity. The most important is that of inclusivity, giving up separation. In order to obtain this, many people will need to relinquish their cherished notions of that which will be, so that the Plan of God can proceed to benefit all of Humanity. He feels that this will be difficult, for certain ideals have been cherished for so long that they are thought to be absolute Truth; when in Truth, they are absolute misconceptions that have been perpetuated in the thought forms of mass consciousness and fueled and energized by fanaticism.

The idea that Christ's crucifixion was to clear the sins of individuals is a misconception. The crucifixion of Jesus was to prove ascension. It is important that we drop our illusions in order to be free to open our hearts to receive the new and to let the Golden Light of the Aquarian Age and the Violet Flame of Transformation and Freedom infuse us.

As this energy progresses in frequency, those beings who refuse change and remain rigid in their erroneous beliefs and refuse to accept anything other than their own point of view will suffer greatly.

Saint Germain says when these rigid ones have reached the point of fanaticism; they have also reached a capability of physical violence, for they are totally controlled by the emotional body to the exclusion of their higher mental faculties. They are totally unpredictable and unreliable and they are ruled by the mass entity rather than by their God Self.

Violent reactions will abound. Centuries of being fed false information will be confronted by truth. Individuals with minds closed to change will rise up against the truth that is now finally being revealed and react violently, demanding that they alone hold the truth.

Visualize the Transmuting Violet Fire acting upon the masses, changing the attitudes of hostility into loving understanding. See it changing resentment into acceptance. Ask that the Will of God be done on the Earth to restore the Divine Plan of the Creator. We can use the Violet Flame as a flaming sword, cutting away hindrances and obstructions to the Divine Plan manifesting in the lives of all Humanity. We are called to use our intention and thought power to manifest these changes. Everything happens through intention and energy follows intention.

The truth of reincarnation, believed in by many of the World, contradicts Christian belief in a heaven and hell and of reward and punishment by God.

You can mentally see yourself giving violet or purple flowers in a vase or Hawaiian lei to someone as an act of offering the Violet Flame of Transmutation and Freedom.

When there is a need for forgiveness for something done in the past, we can transmute the act with the Violet Flame. We can use the Flame of Love to transmute any energy into the energy of Christ Perfection, the Light of Love.

We have lived many lives in far less than perfection. We are now balancing these lives and can speed up the process through the use of the Violet Flame. They can be dissipated and transmuted and the energy released into the Light of Love. Energy which was misqualified by us through ignorance, selfish desires and actions can be cleared by using the Violet Flame. We can clean up our act so to speak. All the energy caught in the astral plane due to our own misqualifications, when set free through transmutation, ascends into our own Causal bodies. Therefore, clearing the astral plane has the multipurpose of reclaiming energy we have misused previously into purified energy for today's use. It is both a service to Humankind and to us.

Our key to service with the Spiritual Hierarchy lies in our ability to be silent and receptive to suggestions from our Higher Selves, which flows from our I AM Presence. We have access to Love, Wisdom and Knowledge beyond our imagining when we access our I AM Presence in meditation.

We are powerful and, at this very crucial point in time, we have the responsibility to show forth as much Light as is Humanly possible. We must seek coordinated effort between our four lower bodies, our Oversouls, Our Christ Self and our I AM Presence to understand our missions within the Spiritual Hierarchy, the Federation and the Divine Plan of the Creator.

Even though many of the energies coming toward the Earth are causing storms where a great deal of negative energy has accumulated, it is also possible for us to use the 21stRay of God to dissipate, dissipate, and dissipate storms. For the Northern Hemisphere we simply call upon the Master Djwhal Khul and the Angel Hippica to orchestrate the Elemental Kingdoms of Fire, Water and Air to dissipate, dissipate, and dissipate any storm we see on a weather forecast or from our own observation in nature. In the Southern Hemisphere we invoke the Master Eufauchia and the Angel Josiah to orchestrate the Elemental Kingdoms of Fire, Water, and Air to dissipate, dissipate, dissipate the storm and move it away from civilization. We can also see rain or snow as a form of the Violet Flame coming to the Earth.

We can also work with the magma of Earth by calling forth the 20th Ray of Earth Magma Control and the Master Latinaous and the Angel Godfrey to calm the magma of Earth. There are 49 Rays of Energy coming to us from the Heart of God for our use to improve conditions on Earth and to transmute negative energies. The Seventh Ray of Divine Magic, Ceremonial Ritual, Transmutation and Freedom is only one of the powerful Rays that have been gifted by God for our use.

If we do not change our ways through our own power of thought and intention, the Elemental Kingdoms will continue to wreak havoc upon the face of the Planet until there is a balance of positive thought and karmic balance. Humans' most positive character and generosity often come to the forefront when there is a disaster and loss. Many people go through life very complacently, worrying, but not doing anything positive until absolutely necessary. We can call forth the Violet Flame and Angels to minister to people experiencing these natural disasters. There are thousands of unemployed Angels waiting to be assigned missions by Humans.

The manuscript of the book *The 49 Rays: Their Meanings and Uses* is available through Amazon.com or may be purchased from Namaste Enrichment Center, Inc. There is also a beautiful deck of cards with this information available from Namaste Enrichment Center, Inc.

There are many aspects of Light, many fractions and refractions which are available for their specific usage. There is the Blue Flame Power to strengthen and purify the will so that the Will of God may be done through us. This is but one of the available facets. There are times when there is a need for the Rose of Love, that soothing and comforting agent which, when it flows through us, brings calm and peace to those near us. There is the Green Emerald Fire, the balancing agent of the Universe with its Divine Healing Powers. It restores the balance within us, bringing things into accord. There is the Yellow Fire of Illumination, of intellect, that opens the door to intuition.

We have tremendous creative power through visualization and imagination and we are asked to perform this service of the use of the Violet Flame for our own benefit of clearing and for all of Humanity. We are to always blaze the Violet Flame to surround us and into everything we see. Even though we may not see the energy, unless we have higher vision, it is there and responds to our call.

It is recommended by Saint Germain that we also repeat this decree three times:

I Am the Violet Flame in action through the World to erase all errors and to break down barriers to Christ Perfection.

Calling forth the Violet Flame is only one of the ways we can help; we can also call forth Great Beings from the Great Central Sun, the Violet Devas, the Elohim, the Spiritual Hierarchy and the members of the Intergalactic Federation who are now stationed around the Earth ready to serve and help. They will respond when they are called into service by us. They do not have permission to intervene in the Human condition unless asked by a Human.

Fanaticism and terrorism will increase until we use our power to transmute and awaken to Truth these beings that are operating from ignorance and fear.

The astral realm and all it contains is a Human creation. It is through this astral realm that we must progress to free ourselves from each of the sub planes within it. We do a service to Humanity and to the planet as a whole if we use conscious effort and directed energy into the astral plane to dispel the residue of what Humanity and we ourselves have added to this astral dimension.

That which has been deposited there is still there. Lost souls, beings who did not make it through into the first level of Heaven, can attach themselves to people choosing to travel in the astral plane out of curiosity.

Now that we are in the Fourth dimension, these lost beings, if they were addicted to a substance or behavior and without a body cannot find relief, are attaching themselves to people who are using their addiction of choice (drugs, food, nicotine, sex, etc.) to get relief. It is important in this Age when we and Earth are moving through the astral plane on our way to the Fifth dimension, vibrationally, that we clean up this effluvia and release these souls by calling upon the Archangel Michael and the Band of Mercy (a group of Angels whose job it is to escort lost souls) to escort anyone we may know of who may be stuck there or just in general ask them to enter the astral plane and rescue any lost souls there. Because we are now within the limits of the astral plane, it is even more important that we continually affirm being surrounded by a shield of Light. Transmuting negative thought forms and releasing wandering entities is important work which we are all capable of performing. Though our actions, the astral plane will become less dense and eventually disappear.

The use of the Violet Flame will come into prominence in the Aquarian Age we have just entered. Those of us who are forerunners and well experienced in the use of the Flame will be laying the cornerstone and foundations for the teachings for the various uses of the Violet Flame. We are the wielders of the Light and it is up to us to consciously direct the Christ Light and the Violet Flame where it will do the most good. The energy that we wield in the name of the I AM Presence affects each and every soul upon the Earth. We have a definite purpose in learning this now and carrying this knowledge forward in our life activities. Many diverse people are being brought together for the purpose of extending this knowledge and utilizing the power of the group for maximum benefit. It is up to each individual to join in collective action of a group that produces magnified results. Now is the time when group effort is to be achieved through conscious effort, dedication and directed will power.

When enough effort is put forth by us it will be as though a weight were lifted from the masses of Humankind. When enough coordinated effort is spent, transmuting the astral levels, the glorious Light of God will shine through and Love will permeate the hearts and minds of Humankind.

Saint Germain suggests using the Violet Flame in the astral plane to diminish those thought forms that are menacing Humankind. Use of the Flame by us can dispel glamour and illusion clouding the minds of Humanity, which is such a hindrance to the Plan of God and the Spiritual Hierarchy.

At this time there is a rising tide, but it is a tide of indecision and it fluctuates between hope and depression.

We are asked to send a Whirlwind of Violet Fire to the United Nations, to governments and individually to the ruling Parliaments and Congresses throughout the planet. We ask the Violet Fire to disintegrate the competition, greed, glamour and illusions that cause legislators to manipulate events, circumstances and conditions to their own selfish ends. This is a powerful activity that can call forth help from Higher Beings to aid the Divine Plan. These Beings can only help if they are asked and called forth by us; this includes the Intergalactic Federation.

When we transmute negative energies, it releases imprisoned Light energies that now may be used for a positive purpose. If we participate, I am assured we will SECURE THE FUTURE OF THE PLANET AND HUMANITY.

We have a responsibility to intensify and magnify and send the Violet Flame into every corner of the Earth where decisions are being made that will affect the Planet and Humanity, such as the election of public officials.

It is recommended that we create a fixed habit of calling forth the Violet Flame. If we do, Saint Germain assures us that progress will be made and results will be forthcoming, visible and tangible, affecting life of all Humankind. We were embodied to do this work of bringing forth the maximum power our bodies can accommodate in the greatest magnitude that we are able to draw forth.

We hold the key to the future within our hearts and minds. If we blaze the Violet Transmuting Flame and see it spreading about us wherever we go, it will be noted and recorded in that our efforts are a part of the work of the Spiritual Hierarchy and it will produce more Light within our Causal Bodies. It is recommended that every time we invoke the Violet Transmuting Flame that we see swirling Violet stardust, scintillating and fiery, blazing and transmuting all within our own auras, blazing and transmuting all that comes in contact with it, and above all see it working its mighty magic within all the seats of government on the Earth.

We are One and this Oneness is the Goal of our evolution, from the lowest, lowliest atom up to the Solar Logos. We are all striving for Oneness. This Oneness can be manifest by daily action and daily living, by constant striving and elimination through the use of this gift of the Violet Fire, in which all petty differences, all minor irritations, disturbances, bigotries, prejudices must be dissolved. For without being dissolved and transmuted by the use of the Violet Flame, there can be no Oneness, no Oneness of Humanity and with no Oneness of Humanity there is no freedom in our future.

The Statue of Liberty Torch is of Violet Fire. See that torch blaze forth to dispel all that is less than God Perfection. This Flame is unceasing and unlimited. You can't wear it out. You can't use it up. It is an inexhaustible supply.

We are the Earthly manifestation of the workings of the Spiritual Hierarchy and they count on us greatly to hold the balance of Light on the Planet. This Flame is the most powerful dynamic activity of God-Love in action that has been manifest upon the Earth plane, and it took many Ages, millennia, for it to develop to the point where you can use it as consciously as you can now.

We can willfully transmute all that is a hindrance to us. This power is inherent within our being. We have only to call it forth. Know this, believe this, use this and see the results.

We can use it in crowds, such as sporting events, concerts, church services; in person or as seen on television and in traffic situations. If used consistently, we can avoid much of the destruction which is now in the offing. If we use it, we alleviate conditions that would be much more drastic without our assistance. We are the outward manifestation on the physical plane of the Spiritual Hierarchy; we are the embodiment of God. We are in whatever location we are living for this purpose. Call it forth every morning and whenever you remember throughout the day. Ask your Higher Self to activate and keep it going all night while your body is asleep.

The Violet Flame is unequaled in its ability to transmute fear and inhibitions. We should use it before an encounter we suspect will be unpleasant or undesirable.

When we talk about the Seventh Ray being the Ray of Ceremonial Ritual and Magic and the Ray of Focus for the Aquarian Age, it is to be understood this includes our postures, flowers, candles, incense, music, rhythm, harmony and blending of higher vibrations with our own. This also includes our clothing and wearing certain colors for specific reasons. Color and the vibrations of colors are extremely important. The clothes we wear, the way we decorate our homes and even how we set and decorate our dining tables is a form of ritual and ceremony.

There is family, group, racial and national karma to be considered when we think of clearing and balancing World karma. The Karmic Board is now available for our use 24/7 to bring situations to them for karmic balance. Approaching the Karmic Board at this time we can relieve huge amounts of accumulated negative karma.

We are transmitters of these higher frequency vibrations and Rays. We are transformers stepping the energy down to the vibration of Humans. We are asked to think of ourselves as Radiant Beings through which the Unlimited Light of the Universe is constantly pouring in through the top of our heads, irradiating our entire being until every atom of our body sings, our body is in harmony with its higher counterparts, and we produce a chord, a musical tone which sends forth Divine Energy. As these Energies, these myriad of atoms of Light, resonate and resound and sing with the joy of being, so this Music of Light/Life cannot be contained within you and it pours forth.

When we are so in tune within ourselves, we are in tune with all the kingdoms of being. We are in tune with the Animal Kingdom and our vibrations are beneficial to the Plant Kingdom. When we are attuned properly, there is a vibratory exchange between you and the Mineral Kingdom. When the balance is complete within the four lower Worlds, then in turn we resonate with the Spiritual Kingdom.

All life is interdependent.

MEDITATION FOR CALLING FORTH THE VIOLET FLAME OF TRANS-MUTATION FOR ALCHEMY

1. I deliberately seal this room on the north, south, east and west. I seal the ceiling and the floor against any negative influence or entity. I deliberately fill this room with the blue light of protection.
2. I call forth and ask for the assistance of the Master Saint Germain and the Violet Flame of Transmutation. I ask the Violet Flame to move through my body and consciousness to transmute any beliefs I hold in limitation or doubt of my abilities to manifest my true heart's desires.
3. I call on the Law of Forgiveness to forgive all my mistakes, discord, problems and limitations, as well as those of all Humankind.
4. Breathing deeply I feel my emotions calming. I feel serene. I feel myself at one with God, at one with the Universe.
5. I decree: I consciously enter and abide within the Heart of the Sacred Fire—the true center of my Being.
6. I AM the Presence of God within the Heart of the Sacred Fire and I speak and command with authority.
7. I AM vested with the Power of the Three times Three. X 3

8. I AM vested with the Power of Transmutation. X3
9. I AM vested with the Power of Precipitation. X3
10. I AM vested with the Power of Levitation.X3
11. I invoke the assistance of the Elemental Kingdom and the energy of Mercury to speed my manifestation.
12. "LET THERE BE LIGHT", I call forth a cloud of undefined infinite energy into a diameter of nine feet around me to intensify my energy field.
13. I now design a mental matrix of what I desire to precipitate. I see the size, color, proportions, substance, density and details of my desire.
14. I state where I wish the manifestation to appear.
15. I ask the Universal Mind to install within the vision of my desire the correct chemical formula for what I desire to create. I visualize the perfection of my design and ask God to correct and perfect any details I have omitted in my design.
16. In the Name of the Presence of God which "I AM" – through the Magnetic Power of the Sacred Fire vested in me I command the appearance of my desire manifested through the Divine Right Action of God now. When you have the visualization clear in your mind state, "IT IS FINISHED! Not my will, but God's will be done." And thereby release the design to the Elementals and the Builders of Form.

Concentration and perseverance are important. Don't give up.

6.

I Am Presence On Supply From the Ascended Masters

The Masters use the term "supply" to mean money and all physical things. We are encouraged by the Masters to make direct contact with our own I AM Presence and to constantly give attention to and send love to our I AM Presence. The Presence is our God aspect. We are encouraged by the Masters to give our I AM Presence dominion over our thoughts, emotions and actions, We have a responsibility to be grateful to our Presence for our life, our body, our freedom of choice, our ability to think, imagine and to create. Intend and imagine your I AM Presence running your life and affairs. Agree to do things God's way. Call your I AM Presence into the physical octave. You are God's Life, God's Energy, and God's directing intelligence if you choose. You must gain mastery over your own concentration and imagining faculty. "Beloved Mighty I AM Presence and Ascended Masters teach me your way of life and focus the Heart Flame from my Higher Mental Body into my physical body now."

The supply for our lives comes from our I AM Presence, from above.

Our I AM Presence was great enough to get us here and to supply us with life with a heartbeat and with the energy we use every moment to breathe. Therefore it is powerful enough to bring us what we require for all our needs and desires. We belong to our I AM Presence and the World belongs to the I AM Presence. It has its own Divine Plan of Its own relationship to the rest of the World. We are responsible for fulfilling a part of the I AM Presence's Divine Plan. We are responsible to fulfill the Divine

Plan our I AM Presence's way.

Not until we have gained control over the feelings in our solar plexus and when we calm the energy in our emotional body and activate the Flame in our Heart and learn to control our Higher Mental Body can the I AM Presence work through our bodies.

The Masters say: *"If you wish to control manifestation begin with control of your attention, an expansion of the Flame in your own heart and then reach up and thank all life above you for the love it has poured into this World, the Ascended Masters, your Beloved Mighty I AM Presence, Angelic Hosts, The Elohim, Cosmic Beings, Great Central Sun, your Galactic Sun and the Creator God of All Universes. Send the Sacred Fires Purifying Love into the World and all life on the Earth to consume hatred, fear, anger and violence.*

"The secret is to begin with Peace and Balance as discord and selfishness block flow. You may call forth to your Beloved Mighty I AM Presence and the Ascended Host from the Heart Flame of my I AM Presence and the Heart Flames of the Seven Mighty Elohim, the Heart Flames of the Ascended Masters and all Cosmic Beings who are always ready to help. Until the attention goes to the Heart Flame of Love's Indestructible Purity and calls It forth into outer physical conditions to hold a balanced flow of everything, your supply and your channels of supply are not permanent nor protected. Pour Sacred Fire Love into all life around you and let its Indestructible Purity go forth to create Balance in the World around you and in return you will receive all good things from the Heart's Flame Sacred Fire Love from your Mighty I AM Presence and the Hearts of the Ascended Host and Hearts of the Seven Mighty Elohim. You must be in control of your own attention."

Call forth the Sacred Fire Love's Indestructible Purity, Balance and Peace and to control physical conditions. Call forth Sacred Fire Love of Indestructible Purity's Protecting Presence around you.

Beloved I AM Presence fill me with and keep me filled with your Heart's Love that holds Balance, inner and outer, wherever I AM and your consciousness in my mind that holds that which is worthy to be made eternal and invincible.

We are invited to demand and command of our Presence what we desire. The Masters desire is for us to become free of all debt and obligations in order to be free to follow the suggestions of our souls and the I AM Presence. We are admonished to discontinue borrowing money because it puts us under the will of the lender. Debt and fear are repellent forces and push away the things we desire. The habit of race consciousness has bound itself to us through debt, doubt, fear and lack of love which makes us slaves.

Demand the Blue Light of Cosmic Christ Purity to shatter the fear of lack within you and compel the love of your I AM Presence to replace it.

It is recommended that we demand and command a limitless supply from our I AM Presence in the amount that is ours by Divine Right. We are to first anchor our attention into our I AM Presence, send love to our Presence and then to imagine, intend and make distinct and definite image of what we desire in order to anchor Light Substance into our design. Everything is made from Cosmic Light Substance. All of what we think of as space is actually Light Substance. Space is not dark. It only appears to us to be dark because it is a frequency of Light that our Human eyes cannot yet register.

Our I AM Presence says, "Love in your feeling World is the magnetic attraction which draws the Universal Cosmic Light Substance into your outer manifestation. Love is the great cohesive power of the Universe. Pour Love into everything. Your feeling about a thing is the enjoyment of it before it manifests. Hold clearly in your mind the sharp, clear picture of what you desire to produce for the constructive activity of fulfilling the Divine Plan and pour your love into it. Love is enjoyment of what the Presence desires to do though you. Use the affirmation: 'Supply, opportunities and all wonderful blessings come to me now from channels I never knew existed.'

"If the attention of the outer self becomes fastened to another's supply with determination to bring it to yourself, even though you are doing something constructive you will fail ultimately even though you draw or pull that thing into your World temporarily. You cannot hold a picture in your mind that interferes with the destiny of another individual or group and expect success. Love alone is the fulfillment of the Law of perfect manifestation in the physical octave. By sending your Love and asking your I AM Presence to produce into your hands and use here in the physical plane in its own way by the Power of Its own Love you give the Presence the open door by which its magnetic currents can draw from many channels more than you can use in the physical octave. Your World belongs to your Presence. Your Presence is an open door into limitless supply."

When we keep our focus on people we are limited, but when we place our attention on our I AM Presence and the Ascended Host we are unlimited.

Bill paying suggested affirmation to I AM Presence: "Show me the most joyful way of obedience to you and most powerful focus of your love to me that brings this into my hands as you want me to have it now. Beloved I AM Presence pay these bills. Keep me happy with your Love pouring through me that whatever is necessary for me to do to pay them, I do through love and all love comes to me to pay them."

Giving Love back to our I AM Presence and enjoyment in fulfilling the Divine Plan keeps the stream of our supply open.

When we have created something we desire to have removed. "Mighty, Beloved I AM Presence forgive me for not obeying you as you take care of me. Please dissolve what I have miscreated and replace it with a thousand times better."

Live in close contact with your I AM Presence. Claim dominion through your I AM Presence over all conditions of discord. Bless everything and everybody you encounter with the fulfillment of the Ascended Masters' Divine Plan and the Love of the "Presence" in All.

Ask your I AM Presence what it desires you to do in the physical octave in the way of physical service in order for what you desire to become an outer manifestation for you.

We can receive Ascended Master Consciousness by asking for it. Harmony must be maintained in our lives for us to become the director of our circumstances. We are to ask our I AM Presence to infuse our desire with the Ascended Master Consciousness, which produces the manifestation more quickly.

Suggested affirmation: "I AM the boundless opportunities required here now. I demand and command boundless wealth from my I AM Presence to come into my use to give me unconditional freedom to accomplish the Divine Plan of my soul."

Spirit says: *"You are the bearers of the Light of Eternity and your destiny is the victory of perfection."*

The Cosmic Beings have created and sustain with perfection Systems of Worlds, Suns and Galaxies. Their love is Perfection, Limitless and all-powerful and eternal everywhere.

The Maha Chohan of the first seven Rays of God is the authority of all Supply to Earth and Guardian of the Treasure House of God's Universe. We can call forth the Cosmic Christ Consciousness energy forth with limitless blessing to the Powers of Nature and the Elementals that carry out the designs of the Maha Chohan.

We can command that our supply as we send it out becomes a being of immortal Love and Light that blesses with Love everything it contacts. We can bless our manifestations to become self-luminous and imperishable in the perfection they produce for us. We are to charge all that comes under our direction with the Ascended Masters' Immortal Love, Purity and Happiness to make it self-luminous.

Life is continually returning to us the energy we sent out to Life with exactly the same qualities we sent it out. We are to bless all of our supply with Love and Perfection and command it into outer action. The more we use the more is given.

"My Beloved Mighty I AM Presence I demand the Immortal Victory of Yourself be made alive in me and be the Flame that blazes through me and compel Victory everywhere in the physical octave where ever I AM."

Spirit says: "*Your Light is like a bridge on which the service of the Masters and their blessing may come into many beings as you are busy with our outer World activities. There must be an up-reaching of some una-scended Humankind in a nation before there is the connection through that permits the Cosmic Love to use its great Powers to affect the many. Every time you send your love to your I AM Presence it draws back more love into the physical octave and it is on the return love from your I AM Presence that the Hierarchy can move into outer action with Cosmic Powers to assist the whole mass of people of a nation or a World.*"

The more certain you are the more Power you can release.

"I command the Power of the Victorious Christ and its Cosmic Light to be made alive in me. I command my Mighty Beloved I AM Presence to clothe me with yourself. I call forth the Ascended Masters' feeling and manifestation move into dynamic service to bless life wherever I AM with fulfillment of the Divine Plan with boundless, unlimited supply."

"Beloved Mighty I AM Presence and the Ascended Host, give me the things from your octave that belong in this World to enable me to fulfill the Divine Plan of my soul."

Interstellar Space is not dark. It is made up of a Light vibration the Human eye can not perceive. Above our power of sight are infinite vibrations in the Universe. We are to reach up vibrationally and ask to learn to do what is greater than what you are doing now. As long as we believe we can't remember our night work we won't. It is based on belief.

What you think you create; what you contemplate you become.

If we contemplate the Ascended Master way of life and begin to love it, feel it, desire it, call it to ourselves we will find many things of perfection from the Ascended Master octave coming into our World and seeking us.

"I command and demand that my Beloved Mighty I AM Presence bring me now the supply of the Universe that is mine by Divine Right into my physical reality. Bring me the boundless supply and see that I do your way of life in the physical World by doing your will here. I ask to express your Divine Plan and to live the way of the Ascended Masters. I ask that you bring this to me now and that I feel it in my physical body."

When there is a problem immediately ask your I AM Presence to place its instantaneous feeling of full solution into the problem.

I call forth the Ascended Masters' Victory of Obedience into everything in this World.

Look at people and trouble grows. Look at God and trouble goes.

Take your mind off people and put it on your I AM Presence. Ask your I AM Presence to give you victory over your selfishness, hatred, greed, jealousy and discord. Ask for the Ascended Masters' protection, Love, victory and supply.

Design what you desire and command energy to come into that form from unlimited Cosmic Substance.

I call forth the Victory of God's control of the Government of America.

I AM Presence forgive all Humankind's wrong and take it out of the Universe now by Your Sacred Fire. I command all energy I have used in the past to be purified now by the Sacred Fire.

I command and demand my freedom from my own habits of discord. I demand freedom from any habit I have that limits me or is destructive.

When a habit disturbs you as that through the Sacred Fire Authority of I AM that I AM, which I AM, I command this habit to stand aside and be annihilated from the Universe while I enter into my permanent association with the perfection of the Ascended Masters' octave of Light.

I ask to be shown the Temples of Sacred Fire and the Magnificence and Beauty of the Ascended Masters' octave of Light.

I demand that perfection come into me and fill my World that Its Light may forever lead all Light into greater Light and out of distress and discord.

At night we are admonished to say: "Beloved Mighty I AM Presence, with Your Power of Sacred Fire, I demand my attention this next day be held on the Perfection of Your World; and I demand Your perfection blaze in, through and around me and fill my World with Your Love and Power of the Sacred Fire."

Don't say I will; say I do give my attention and obedience to my Higher Mental Body.

Demand annihilation of negative thoughts.

When you see a situation that needs correction say: "Mighty Beloved I AM Presence blaze enough Violet Consuming Flame energy into this situation to wipe out what is wrong and to replace it by what is right to fulfill Your Divine Plan."

We've got to have the Divine Plan fulfilled in us if we are going to be healed permanently. The healing is not just a matter of the control of atomic structure of the flesh, because the cause of the discord is in the emotional body and the mind. Demand with fierce determination.

The Spirit says: "If you only knew what your feelings could do for you, you would be free in a few hours."

I demand the breaking of every habit of thought, feeling and spoken word that accepts any lack or limitation in me and in my World.

Every time we use supply in the outer World we can train our minds to receive a larger supply from our I AM Presence. Acknowledge your I AM Presence as the giver of your security.

Whenever money goes out from you and you use it in the outer World, send it forth to bless and fulfill the Divine Plan; and immediately, when you send it out, turn to your Presence and ask for supply ten or a thousand times more. The same thing is true of our health. After we use energy we are to call forth more energy from our I AM Presence.

Our life is loaned to us and contains the qualities and activities of the Great Central Sun at the center of the Milky Way. The Great Central Sun gives energy to our Galactic Sun administered by Helios and Vesta and they give energy to the Great Central Sun at the core of the Earth. Each of us is a Sun magnet and a Sun presence.

We can only gain mastery by expansion of our own Heart's Flame by letting the Light of Its Love go before us and fill the World around us, and recognizing the boundless supply of perfection from the Ascended Masters octave of Light.

We can ask for greater perfection, greater happiness, greater blessings, and greater beauty to all Life.

There is nothing as stifling on the Earth as selfishness.

I call forth the I AM boundless supply of perfection from the Ascended Masters' octave of Light.

There are Seven Mighty Elohim of Creation who are Builders of the manifest Universe. If it were not for the Great Cosmic Beings of the Spiritual Hierarchy and the Angelic Realm who constantly guard the Life of this World, there would be nothing to sustain Humankind. Send Love first to your Beloved Mighty I AM Presence and the Ascended Host who have created and sustained the systems of the Worlds, to all Beings and Powers of Nature and to other Planets and Star Systems and to all Cosmic Beings.

Send the Flame of Love up to your I AM Presence and to the Ascended Hosts, the Seven Mighty Elohim of Creation, the Cosmic Christ Illuminating Love.

Ask for Ascended Master Consciousness and command what you desire to come into your physical World.

I AM the Sacred Fiery Christ Purity and Eternal Command for all that is wrong to cease to be. Use your Cosmic authority and your Freewill.

I ask the Light and Sacred Fire from my Higher Mental Body and the Mighty Beloved I AM Presence of each Life Stream to expand within the outer self and release the Powers of Life that produce perfection and perfection manifestation.

"I call forth to my Beloved Mighty I AM Presence and the Ascended Host to charge into my body and the outer World conditions the Cosmic Light Substance that cannot be requalified by any Human consciousness. I call forth more and more of this to come into the physical octave of Earth to be the Strength and Protection in and around all that is constructive."

The energy the Dark Brotherhood can use is the atomic structure and feeling world of the physical bodies of Humankind on Earth. They cannot use the Ascended Master octave or the Cosmic Light Substance of space.

The Light of God never fails.

The Light of God that never fails is the Sacred Fire of the Great Central Sun and also from the Heart Flame of every Ascended Master and Cosmic Being.

I call the Cosmic Light Substance into the substance of the physical World to be the Immortal Purity and the constructive Power and Qualities that produce manifestation that is perfect.

I call forth the Ascended Masters' Illuminating Strength of the Cosmic Light into my mental and feeling World and into the mental and feeling World of others and into the atmosphere, the Powers of Nature and the Forces of the Elements. These Infinite Powers of Light are gifts from the Great Central Sun. All things are made of Cosmic Light Substance.

I call forth to my Mighty Beloved I AM Presence to bring Its Light and Love into and around me. I ask my Higher Mental Body to draw the Cosmic Light Substance into me for me to use the Master Powers of my own Mighty I AM Presence in my outer World.

I call forth the Fiery Christ Miracle Mantel of Love's Mastery to come into the physical condition to compel perfection.

All thought, feeling, spoken word and act produces some kind of manifestation.

I call forth Love from the Sacred Fire of the Great Central Sun.

The Divine Plan must be filled with the Cosmic Light Substance. Concentrate the Cosmic Light Substance into the condition in order to produce the thing into manifestation.

Ask your Beloved Mighty I AM Presence to call forth the Cosmic Light Substance into a tube of Light around you for protection.

Great Cosmic Beings created the Earth from the Divine Plan of the Creator God and sustain and produce the Powers of Nature upon the Earth. The systems of the World and Universe are created of Cosmic Light Substance.

I call forth the Ascended Masters' unlimited power, feeling and strength of Cosmic Light Substance consciousness into my I AM Presence for us of the Master Powers of manifestation.

Cosmic Light Substance can be called forth into the physical to become whatever we need to fulfill the Divine Plan.

I call forth the Cosmic Light Substance and Inner Essence of the boundless supply from the Ascended Masters' octave of Light.

I call forth to my Mighty I AM Presence and the Ascended Host for unlimited supply of Cosmic Light Substance into my physical World. I demand that everything in my being and World be forever charged with the Ascended Master Sacred Fire Prevention of all wrong; then my I AM

Presence can trust me with unlimited supply.

I demand the Sacred Love of the Sacred Fire's Cosmic Light Substance and boundless supply of every good thing that forever produces perfection and prevents wrong into my activities.

I demand Eternal, Indestructible Protection around my fulfillment of the Divine Plan for my life, the nation and Humankind.

When we think we need money in reality we need the expansion of the Flame in our own Heart and the Light Substance of the Ascended Masters' octave and the flow of the Luminous Energy from the Great Central Sun Magnet.

We can call forth the Ascended Masters' Fiery Christ Blue Lightening Protection and Purity.

We are responsible for everything we create good or otherwise.

Send Love to your Beloved Mighty I AM Presence and ask It to fill your life with Love and what fulfills the Divine Plan for your life.

Earth's atmosphere is loaded with Electronic Force, Energy, Substance, Intelligence and Ideas.

Anything that is wrong is a lack of Love and Light.

We are to bring into America the Sacred Fire's Indestructible Purity and Cosmic Light Substance.

Through my Beloved Mighty I AM Presence and all the Ascended Host, I AM the All-Christ Indestructible Mastery over every Human condition.

The Fiery Christ Blue Lightening Purity can annihilate what is wrong.

I ask my Beloved Mighty I AM Presence and the Ascended Host to furnish my World with health and financial abundance from the Ascended Masters' octave that is indestructible and untouchable by Human miss creation.

I call forth Cosmic Light Substance from the Ascended Masters' octave and the Power and Sacred Fire Love from the Seven Mighty Elohim of Creation to fill everything in me and my World with indestructible harmony, protection and illumination and supply of every good thing.

Beloved Mighty I AM Presence hold Divine Justice and Balance within me.

Don't fight against conditions call forth the Violet Flame of Transmutation. Pour the Violet Flame of Transformation, the Fiery Christ Blue

Lightening Purity into the outer physical World conditions.

I AM Indestructible Purity and consume all discord around me.

I ask my Beloved Mighty I AM Presence to fill me with your Sacred Fire Purifying Power, Purifying Wisdom, Purifying Balance, and hold eternal control over everything in my World and being.

Beloved Mighty I AM Presence and Ascended Host Indestructible Balance of Love, Wisdom, Power, Divine Justice, Sacred Fire Purity, Indestructible Sacred Fire Love and Cosmic Light Substance and hold that within me in Perfect Balance to create permanent supply in my physical World of every good thing.

Fiery Christ Truth and Illuminating Consciousness can't come until intellectual consciousness makes the call.

Think and be grateful for all your Mighty I AM Presence has already given you.

I ask my Beloved Mighty I AM Presence and the Ascended Host to enfold me in the Mighty I AM Miracle Mantle of Love's Eternal Divine Justice and Balance and to control all circumstances around me.

I call Cosmic Power, Sacred Fire, and the Violet Transmuting Flame into myself, my body, my city, state and country.

I ask my I AM Presence to assist me to control my attention and ability to concentrate.

If you desire to be free of discord, stretch your mental muscles and think about the Magnificent Love that sustains the Infinite Manifestations of Worlds and Cosmic Systems in Perfect Divine Order and Balance. Call forth to your Beloved I AM Presence and the Ascended Host and to the I AM Presence of everyone embodied on Earth. Call to the Source of Unconquerable, Limitless, invincible, Victorious Love, the Sacred Fire Love of every life stream embodied on Earth, the Sacred Fire of the Great Central Sun, the Sacred Fire Love of the Physical Sun and the Sacred Fire Love that keeps this World sustained, keeps it in its orbit, keeps the Powers of Nature growing upon it the things to sustain you and by which you are enabled to embody here to manifest as a Human being and to draw forth life into all the outer activities to fulfill the Divine Plan.

Fill yourself with the I AM Presence Sacred Heart Fire and ask the I AM Presence to pour forth into the condition that is wrong in the World the Sacred Fire Purity Love, Peace, Forgiveness, and Divine Mercy, which enables discord to be consumed.

Only when the attention goes to manifestation before it goes into the Realm of Cause, the I AM Presence, is discord created.

I call forth to my I AM Presence and the Ascended Host to fill me with whatever is necessary for this day to be filled with all good things.

I AM the Ascended Master's Law of Forgiveness and the Consuming Flame of all inharmonious action in Human consciousness. I call forth Christ's Blue Lightening Purity and the Violet Flame of Transmutation into destructive conditions to annihilate with Love, Forgiveness and Mercy to Life.

Ascended Masters can only do for Humankind what they can do through Humankind.

Once a day say: "I AM my Beloved I AM Presence and the Ascended Master's Law of Forgiveness and Consuming Flame of all inharmonious action Human consciousness, and I send it into life everywhere on this Earth; it forgives all discord by filling it with and covering it over with the Violet Flame of Transformation and the Fiery Christ Blue Lightening Indestructible Purity that consumes all evil, all lack and limitation everywhere throughout the World forever. I call forth the Violet Flame of Transformation and the Fiery Christ Blue Lightening Indescribable Purity and Peace to prevent all wrong."

The Masters say: The Heart's Flame of the Seven Mighty Elohim can release more Power into physical conditions than Humankind's comprehension can possibly understand, so through your decrees give the Herculean Elohim Heart Flame control of everything and everybody within America. It can only come into outer physical conditions by Human conscious command to purify and cause peace in the outer."

We are to get in the habit of seeing Light Rays go forth to fulfill our decrees.

I ask to use the Ascended Master consciousness of Supply to bring through my Mighty Beloved I AM Presence the supply that is mine by Divine Right now.

Beloved Mighty I AM Presence fill me with what you know enables me to precipitate directly from the Universal what you know I now need to help myself and others.

We are admonished to hold a picture of the Ascended Masters and the Seven Mighty Elohim in our forehead and our heart and imagine it in the forehead of everyone we contact and to ask our I AM Presence to amplify the Flame in our heart and to pour it our through our hands to create perfection everywhere. The action of our hands is governed entirely by the Heart Flame of our Beloved I AM Presence.

My Beloved Mighty I AM Presence and Ascended Host are first in my life this day and forever.

7.

Channeling From Saint Germain Through bj King

APRIL- MAY 1992

Everywhere there is chaos and confusion in the minds of Humans. To project thoughts of peace and contentment is a worthy cause, but even greater is to project the energy of clarity and hope. Humanity is suffering from lack of hope. Contentment, true contentment, not a momentary lack of struggle, can only come to one who knows the truth of their being as a divine aspect of God. Lack of understanding of truth of origin and true current definition of one's Self is critical to the survival of the species and Earth and needs to be the immediate focus of all spiritual teachers. To be, as one was designed to be, is to be consciously connected to the Source, one's Creator and the sustainer of each individual as their own soul.

To believe and comprehend this as possible should become not unique but an accepted fact of life as it once was before Humans were taken over by their belief in falling from grace as is taught by your Bible. The ego created by Humans wants each Human to believe they are temporary and only physical so the ego can enjoy the confusion and attempt to employ fear in order to dissuade the Human from remembering its origins and true purpose for each incarnation. The truth of each flame of life in each heart is to be revealed, enlarged, identified and used in the service of the Divine Plan of the Creator God through connecting to Infinite Intelligence.

To realize the nature of truth consists of what one is ready and willing to hear, know and understand. When the truth appears in one's life through something read, through a conversation or the voice of another, or through a simple thought that comes into one's mind while observing nature, the moment is holy-wholly. It comes from acknowledging and connecting even momentarily with Oneness; with the body and mind acknowledging even momentarily that they are a part, an aspect of truth of the Oneness of Creation. Each time this happens to an individual, it adds a spark of the awareness to the collective of Human consciousness.

The power of accepting oneself as a part of Oneness of the Universe and beyond as the affirmation we have given states is unlimited: "I AM God operating through this personality for the benefit of Earth, all life on the Earth and beyond. This is the truth of who I AM."

It is suggested that we intend the highest level of our Oversoul to be our receptionist or gatekeeper, keeping us connected only to our soul guidance and keeping all else that is not of our soul's mission away from us.

Teaching about the gatekeeper is one of the most important concepts to teach at this time. The authority of the gatekeeper is to censor, but also to bring forward information designed for a specific individual's under-standing. This is a divine blessing when it is consciously established. The gatekeeper can bring information from members of one's family and friends who have transcended death into other dimensions when the soul deems it advantageous to the being's evolution, but usually the information imparted needs to come from a higher frequency than the recently departed from the physical plane.

Transcendence of thought and intention is important. To transcend what has seemed mundane, like chores, to intending to be God doing the activity whether it is indoors or out is what is expected of Humans. One must transcend thoughts of lack, doubt, confusion, and ill health by control of thoughts and emotions. All must transcend attitudes of unworthiness into knowing you are aspects of God and therefore worthy of all your heart desires. What your heart desires is your soul's desire. What your ego desires are things that by comparison with others makes you look better and successful.

Belonging is for the purpose of use for the furtherance of your goal or soul's mission. This does not mean you should be frugal; it means to stay conscious of spending asking: Why do I desire this object, opportunity or action? Is it my ego or my soul? Often you postpone purchasing because you do not feel the purchase is necessary. That is your frugal, responsible, fear nature kicking in to convince you to restrain because you question, "Where is the next money coming from and when?" You think this rather than thinking it is on its way to you. You deserve abundance and opulence.

If you've never experienced these you may question: Why me? Why now? The answer is because you are beginning to understand that just being conscious deserves reward, knowing and expressing as the truth of who you are as an aspect of the Creator.

I often struggle between logic, efficiency and letting go to Divine timing. I desire to be in alignment with the Divine Plan, but I get impatient when things take longer than I think they should. I do not experience God being logical or efficient and this often causes me to feel frustrated. When this happens I try to focus on and do something physical like clean the house or work in the yard.

Finding one's place in the overall scheme of things usually brings a sense of peace and satisfaction. Utilizing what you have learned is more important than constantly seeking more information through reading or attending lectures or conferences. Being instead of doing is the key to a successful spiritual life. Many feel they have too much to lose through surrendering their body back to their soul. We never and the soul never takes a person's Freewill. Choice is always left to the mind and heart of the individual. We and your souls provide suggestions based on our experience and the knowledge we have of the Big Picture at any given time. If you can trust us, trust your soul; know there are reasons beyond your present knowing and understanding that affect the bigger picture that make some choices unwise or inappropriately timed.

Respect for convention is not the way of a mystic. Mysticism is spontaneous and without borders, having no rules other than those you make for yourself. Do not harm anyone or anything. Be brave and confident and laugh a lot about the chaos and confusion of life. Try this out. You believe order is necessary and it is. The Universes are based on order. Chaos is an illusion perpetrated by minds that unfold and refold thought without witnessing the overall pattern of beingness. Time is an illusion; Humans created from interacting with the Sun and Moon and designing a pattern to their own rhythm. The overall objective of all is expansion, not of girth, but of consciousness.

Everything spiritual happens as a result of intention and imagination. Imagination is a spiritual gift to Humans from the Creator. When one wishes a thing, it is easy to avoid action. When a Human intends a thing they normally follow through with action, but to actually intend a thing, one must imagine oneself doing it and following through with action.

Spiritual work is the same. A person can think about raising their vibration through breath, food nourishment and imagination and never do anything deliberately about following through with action. People are often too busy to breathe consciously, too busy to meditate, too busy to imagine traveling out of body, too busy to pray, too busy to exercise, too busy to be truly spiritual, too busy to prepare for life beyond the physical. Imagine, intend and follow through with action.

Formal training to become a mystic is normally accomplished through intensive training by a Master/disciple relationship. The time for such arduous and time consuming training has passed. The Spiritual Hierarchy is facing time constraints in relationship to the evolution of Humans and the Earth. We need to get a larger percentage of Humanity into conscious communication and cooperation with Divinity and the Divine Plan of the Creator for Humanity and the Earth. The evolution energetically of Earth's ascension is in process and therefore Humans must raise their vibrations also to make this transition with the Earth. One for all and all for one is to be acknowledged because it is a reality.

When Humans bother to study the history of Earth and Humanity they come in contact with facts and progression of evolution of their species and changes, dramatic changes, in the surface of the Earth, the shifting of the Earth's axis and changes in the typography of the crust of the Earth. The Earth has been more or less stable during the past century; Humans have become complacent and have not accepted their responsibility for cooperating with nature, the Elementals and Earth. Humans have been busy attempting to control nature and the Earth rather than cooperating with her. Humans can assist in their own evolution and the evolution of the galaxy, but first they must learn to control themselves and to use the powers gifted to them by their Creator, the power of thought, intention, imagination and action. When these are aligned with a goal, magic, or what Humans perceive as magic, happens.

Control of thought, control of energy, constructive use of imagination are required to assist evolution and to change the outcome for Earth and all species of life on the Earth. Think on these things.

Humming is a great way to raise the vibration of the body as well as conscious breathing.

10-11-04

Soul infusion of the personality, which implies giving all personal choice the opportunity to be "run by the soul" so to speak, is the wisest choice at this time. The reason is that karma is now more instantaneous. If choices are made by the personality alone, without soul consideration, or soul consultation, the choices can result in dire consequences or considerable inconvenience to the personality, because of the Law of Karma within the Aquarian Age. When an Age is reached on the Earth that does not allow for the carrying of accumulated karma from one lifetime to the next, such is the Aquarian Age negative consequences begin to happen rapidly as a result of decisions being made, let's say politically, that are not well thought out or "soul considered" by those making the choices.

It is perhaps easy to imagine creating an event in one's life as a result of personal choice, but less easy to imagine creating an event as a result of avoiding choice. When we decide not to decide, we put all choices in the realm of possibility, but we also put that choice out to the choices of mass consciousness rather than giving that choice to our souls. Random choice, made at the discretion of mass consciousness, comes with karma attached to it immediately. Conscious choice, on the other hand, comes with no karma if the choice is made from the level of the soul and the personality combined, because the possibilities of karma are quantified at the time the decision is made and the consequences, if there are to be any, are markedly exempt from retribution by the soul.

Certain actions, when made at the soul level, are allowed by the soul for the purpose of growth for those surrounding the person taking the action. Such is the case with Edward's death and that of your Mother (bj's mother in this case). Personal choice, when made from the level of the soul, is not exempt from consequence, but is quantified in relationship to the good it can cause in the majority rather than in the personality of one person.

Judgment and fear are the culprits of most decisions. Many people make their decisions based on what others will think of them if they take one action as opposed to another. They either fear the judgment of others or fear the action of others as a result of their own choice or actions. When a choice is made from the level of the personality only, it is usually made from fear of judgment or fear of consequences, not from the level of pure choice to cause a deliberate intended outcome.

The difference between deliberate choice and choices that call for retribution, or what you call karma, is choice made by you and your soul for the purpose of soul growth or manifestation by design. If you choose to manifest a condition in your life, or an object, and this is seen by the soul as a possibility of producing soul growth there will be no negative consequences to suffer. If however, one attempts to accomplish something on *their own, without deliberately consulting the assistance of their soul, they put themselves in a position of accepting the karmic consequences that will come as a result of the actions connected to the choice.*

You will begin to see examples of what I AM explaining within the next three days.

Now we request that you sleep again. Thanks.

6-17-07

The truth of the power of thought lies in observation of the product created by the thoughts. Observation of thought, awareness of the nature and source of the thought is the first step to enlightenment, the first step to self-realization. Prepare your mind, control your mind through practice of deliberate repetitive projection of desired thoughts. Accumulate an arsenal of desired thoughts to counter balance any negative thoughts you might observe in your mind or your speech.

Adonai
6-19-07
Hawaii

Within the Federation, the Councils are divided into 12, 7 and 9. The members of the Councils each elect a Chief of the Council. The representatives of each Council have accrued responsibilities as a result of their previous actions and activities. In your physical forms you may not be aware of your participation with these various Councils as they have a calling toward the resolution or enhancements of certain aspects or sectors of the Human evolutionary experience. Today's Council meets to bring about additional pressure through your aspects to further reveal the deceptiveness of religious groups and beliefs especially those known to you as Catholicism and Fundamentalism. The issues of lack of respect for the Feminine Consciousness of God as developed through Catholicism, as well as the errors perpetrated by certain groups determination to literally translate that which is known as the Bible. *This added pressure to reveal these discrepancies is needed at this time especially after the transition of the one known as Jerry Farlwell. More will be given to you as your mission progresses and as this Council reports your response to vibrationally higher Councils than those with whom you are now familiar and now work. Adonai*

January 5, 2016 Tuesday 9:35 a.m.

St Germain here - you have raised your consciousness stream to reach into the 10th dimension and the consciousness of Ascended Masters. As was predicted to you in 1986, you had volunteered at the level of your soul to bring my messages and consciousness to Humanity and to the physical plane of Earth, starting with explaining the now available Violet Flame of Freedom and Transmutation. I now offer it to all of Humanity for transmutation of negative thought forms and effluvia surrounding and held captive in the Earth's atmosphere. Each individual who learns of this Flame of Purification is qualified to call upon the use of the flame to transmute discord and discordant thinking. As you requested the dispensations from the Karmic Board December 31st you can request and wield massive amounts of the Violet Flame Fire to bring under control the rampant thoughts and activities of gangs, terrorists and warring factions upon the Earth's surface. Your authority is now enforced to present these messages to Humanity. Adonai, Dear Sister of the Flame. I remain your servant, St. Germain.

January 6, 2016 9:32 a.m.

Becoming an Everyday Mystic is a title that will catch the attention of many and the steps to becoming a mystic will seem doable to those who are ready to expand and live from their center. You are guided even when it seems as if you are not. It is good and important that you alternate from stillness within you to connection to your soul and its suggestions. Adonai, Dear One.

January 7, 2916 Thursday 9:34 a.m.

A broken bone in a Human releases consciousness stored there from previous incarnations and can be accepted by the conscious mind of the life form that is conscious enough to accept this as a reality. The initiation you allow to be performed through you to unblock the spiritual secrets stored in a person's knees who have agreed to bring these secrets back to Earth is an invaluable service, even though your ego took a backseat to your soul for you to agree to get down on the floor to perform the toning into their knees. Registering your resistance and uncertainty about channeling for the Ascended Masters is noted. As have been other services asked of you through the years, this is just another level of service, one you have worked for and qualified to perform for us. I remain your Champion and Brother of the Heart. St. Germain. Adonai, Dear Sister of the Flame.

January 8, 2016 Friday 9:30 a.m.

Time is of the essence for reviewing the previous lessons and getting them ready for publication. You will know the correct order of the chapters as we will assist. The one you are working on now will be closer to the beginning than the end as will be the one on dimensions, planes and frequencies and bodies. Thanks, Adonai, Dear One.

January 9, 2016 Saturday 9:30 a.m.

Help with aberrant weather conditions is available to Humans who know about and understand the Rays and the use of the Violet Flame to dissolve the collected negative thought forms and the 21st Ray of Climate Control to seek assistance to orchestrate the Elementals of Earth, Air, Fire, Water and Ether. The use of both these tools, as well as asking Angels to remove the energy of the negative thought forms, can stop some of the potential weather patterns that can cause catastrophes--the same way you did in Minneapolis to circumvent the potential flooding of the Mississippi River. We were not allowed by Cosmic Law to warn you prior to the flooding of the Illinois River or the Missouri River. Thank you for your service to Humanity by making the information about the Rays available to Humanity. Adonai, Dear One.

January 10, 2016 Sunday 9:30 a.m.

Changing the way you feel about your assignments and responsibilities will motivate you to be more focused in your responsibilities. The writing you've done can be useful to many more than can be exposed to it as the lessons we've given. Make more time in your schedule to concentrate on getting it ready to be presented as a book possibly to Hay House. Adonai, Dear One.

January 11, 2016 Monday 9:30 a. m.

St. Germain here, what you have been reading of my Violet Flame Fire of Transmutation in the Gnosis and the Law will give you a deeper understanding of the service you can perform through its use and by calling on my service to clear the negative thought forms and the effluvia which has engulfed the Earth. Explaining this in detail with specific prayers, decrees or wording will be one of the future assignments. These decrees have previously been given to Humanity through the I AM organization. I will lead you to the ones most effective for this Age of Invocation and Ceremonial Magic. It is not necessary to use a forceful voice to qualify the decree only the heartfelt intention to assist in the clearing and transmutation. I remain your servant and friend. St. Germain. Adonai, Dear One.

January 12, 2016 Tuesday 9:34 a.m.

In regard to the Retreat Temples, it will be useful to make this information available on your blog as well as to the students of the Mystery School and to offer the idea of groups meeting on the 15th of each month to activate the flame within each retreat. You are authorized, by me, to use the map of the retreats in your lesson and publication. I ask you to glean from other publications where I have already written what is appropriate to be released at this time to Humanity. I remain your servant, Saint Germain. Use the Violet Fire of Freedom to free yourself. Adonai, Dear One.

January 13, 2016 Wednesday 9:30 a.m.

Write to Laynie and Duane Gibson and send the written meditation for entering the Royal Teton Retreat. The foundation of spiritual work history is recorded in the Gnosis and the Law and most of the descriptions of the current Hierarchy are accurate. When you write about it, who does what, we will tell you of their current assignments. Adonai, Dear One. I remain Saint Germain.

January 15, 2016 Friday 9:30 a.m.

Write to Laynie and Marie Commiskey. To understand dimensional life one must also understand vibrational frequency. The term dimension is not a place or space, but just a frequency of vibration. All is happening simultaneously very much like radio and television channels are picked up by radio and television receivers turned to different frequencies of broadcasts. The difference is that those of us who reside in these various frequencies have the mental capabilities to cause a thought form to be lowered from our dimension into your physicality.

To precipitate as you have witnessed before with the stones. Practice, Dear One. It will be so. Adonai, Dear Sister of the Flame.

January 16, 2016 Saturday 9:30 a.m.

Dear One, I see you are preparing to teach the calling forth of the Violet Flame of Freedom and Transmutation. The necessary or preferred decrees are in the decree books you have had for several years. I acknowledge your petition for precipitation of the paid deed to the property you now inhabit free of debt. The use of the Violet Flame each evening for beings to clear the effluvia of the day from their energy bodies makes it possible for them to ascend to higher realms while they sleep. Using the Flame in service to clearing the Astral Plane of negative or discordant energy is also a service we request now of Humanity. This message and the information you have gleaned from your reading will help many to understand their spiritual responsibility to Humanity and Earth and how to most effectively perform this service. I remain your faithful servant. Saint Germain, Dear Sister of the Flame. Adonai, Dear One.

January 17, 2016 Sunday 9:30 a.m.

Today let us talk about the foundation of wisdom necessary for a person to evolve into a useful instrument of service to the collective of Humanity and the Hierarchy of your Universe. It is not necessary or required of an individual to know and understand all those who are assigned and hold positions within the Spiritual Hierarchy of the Universe within which you reside. It is enough for an individualized life stream to believe they have energy bodies beyond their physical bodies, to respect and control these bodies and to understand the Laws that keep the Universe intact and on purpose. The reason for intellectual understanding to qualify an individual is so that their participation can be conscious and controlled not just by their mind, but also by their heart and feeling nature. To participate consciously in calling forth energy, qualifying it and sending it forth to create cause and result is what is most called for in a participant.

To understand the use of fiats and decrees brings an individual into more usefulness to their own soul, to the collective of Humanity, the Earth and to those beyond the Earth operating in the larger Cosmos of the Universe. The work is not difficult, time consuming or required to be done at the same time daily. Devotion, intention and desire to be of service to the collective are what are called for. You are considering creating a group activity for decreeing and understanding decrees in the future when and if your own energies are promised to you for this endeavor.

Adonai, Dear Sister of the Flame.

January 19, 2016 Tuesday 9:27 a.m.

To reassure you, we are working to create your desired result for ownership of the property you now inhabit. Your practice of precipitation ritual is important to prove to yourself that the method works to move you to begin to teach others this method. You have begun to accept that the responsibility of being in contact with us will not interfere as much as you thought with your daily routine. You are a blessing. Be well. Enjoy. Adonai, Dear One.

January 20, 2016 Wednesday 9:30 a.m.

Sending the decree books and precipitation formula to your friends is a good start in our project to bring the funds you desire to own the property you inhabit. Would this be where you desire to live were unlimited funds made available to you? (Yes, but I would upgrade parts of it and provide housing for others of my friends, family and other people and sponsor scholarships to people who desire further education and travel to places my soul deems important to work for the Spiritual Hierarchy and the Federation.)

You are to evolve even more than you are to eventually qualify for your ascension. (I certainly don't feel qualified for ascension. What would I need *to do?) More service, less entertainment. (Ha! Then give me more stamina and mental clarity to last all day.) Do the exercises and decrees and the nutrition. Focus, Focus, Focus. Adonai, Dear One. I remain your faithful servant Saint Germain.*

January 21, 2016 Thursday 9:34 a. m.

Who I was in history as you are reviewing in the current volume does not mean anything. Only today matters and what we can accomplish together. The research you have done will be important in writing, but as we did when you were writing of the Rays pages may appear as if they have been stored for a long season and will appear among your papers. We also now have the ability to insert certain information into your computer as it becomes necessary from time to time. The authenticity of the information as coming from a higher vibrational source will be without question. You have become less skeptical, which serves our purpose for cooperation, and following examples or suggestions will become ever increasingly important to our mission. Do not concern yourself with the opinions of others. Be content with your own knowingness. Retire earlier and arise earlier when it suits you. You are reforming your reality, which is no small thing. The evidence of truth is on its way. Be still, be aware, be kind and know that always the right things will be known by you. The ritual requirements are now accurate and ready for publication on your blog with the food blessing, which is of extreme importance now, because your food supply is heavily contaminated. You are the source of your own joy. Make use of your gifts to bring yourself into a happier frame of mind. Adonai, Dear One, I remain your friend and confidant, Saint Germain.

January 22, 2016 Friday 9:30 a.m.

Attending the gazing will help your body to adjust more comfortably to this frequency. The more we connect the stronger the connection will be and the happier your body will be. Groat is a form of wheat like oats, but of a different grain family. Barley for you would be comparable. The issue of diet is not as important as the consciousness of the food, which is why the food blessing given to you is so useful. Think of your desire already fulfilled and do not focus on how you are going to cause it to happen. We are working to arrange various avenues of possibility by giving certain individuals oppor-tunity to serve. Adonai, Dear One, I remain Saint Germain.

January 23, 2016 Saturday 9:30

It is not required that you host the gazing, but you do need to be present for several sessions to heal your body and continue to raise your body's vibration to make these energy transfers easier for your body. The will to do the inconvenient thing is important in one who chooses to serve their soul. Your aloneness when others have partners is deliberate. As you know we were unable to find a willing participant to accomplish the goal for you to do your mission in tandem with another. You are unique and your gift of telepathy is special. Your ability to read large quantities of information and sort through for the nuggets of truth to present to today's students who are ready to know more of the truth is what we need now to further our plan of educating the masses that we exist and are willing to help Humanity and the Earth to survive the shift of the Earth's vibration to take her to her rightful place in the galaxy and Universe. Your talents will be invaluable in the service of making as you call it the Reader's Digest condensed version of spiritual knowledge available to those who seek to know more. Adonai, Dear One, I remain your faithful servant Saint Germain.

January 24, 2016 Sunday 9:30 a.m.

The wealth of the Ascended Masters is available to those who choose dispensing wealth as a part of their path, their learning experience. Your consciousness is focused on service. Service through wealth is possible, but it requires extreme focus and discernment of the will of the Creator and the soul of the individual you desire to help. (Do you feel I am not qualified to administer wealth?) The question is not your qualification, but would this action become your focus rather than teaching by example? (Adminis-trating wealth spiritually, it seems to me, is one of the causes of most of the difficulty currently on the planet; so why wouldn't you using my conscious-ness to administrate physical wealth through me not be something that would be useful to you?) Use your emotion to quantify wealth and we will work toward that action. Adonai, Dear One, I remain your faithful servant and friend, Saint Germain.

January 26, Tuesday 930 a.m.

Teaching mysticism is the goal to be in constant awareness of one's I AM Presence and willingness to pursue the suggestions or guidance given through the stream of consciousness given down by the I AM Presence, the true owner of the body and consciousness of each individualized expression of God.

Through the actions of following the I AM's suggestions, the individual develops wisdom. The consciousness expands and the individual becomes at one with higher beings as you have.

The process of surrender, awareness of one's thoughts and feelings are the first steps. Developing control of the mind, the thoughts and feeling nature are required of one who desires to become a mystic.

Anyone can develop psychic abilities such as clairvoyance, clairaudience, telepathy, clairsentience, but only one who truly surrenders their body, mind and emotions to their I AM Presence is to be considered a mystic. A mystic's true intention is to be in direct communication with their soul, their I AM Presence, God at all times and in all places. The usual progression of a soul only moves from psychism to mysticism later in life when one tires of dabbling in spiritual practices and becomes serious about completing their soul's mission; then and only then is the connection made and strengthened with their I AM Presence in a permanent and conscious way. Then the real work of the soul accomplishment can begin; when the ego moves aside and the soul is invited to inhabit the body and act through the body.

Your desire to have ownership and sovereignty of the property is not just the desire of your ego and emotions; it is a true desire of the soul. Adonai, Dear One.

January 27, 2016 Wednesday 9:30 a. m.

Transcending poverty consciousness into the consciousness of wealth and opulence is within a category of miracles. Individuals who have withstood limitation for lifetimes can hardly be expected to instantly receive wealth and understand its utilization. Feelings of self-worth are necessary first and foremost. Action to accumulate is not as necessary as recording information pertaining to its utilization. The foundation of physical wealth is based on a principle of or foundation of degree of service to natural intelligence. (I'm not sure what that means?) Training and skill in utilizing large portions of wealth is not as necessary as the feeling or desire to be of service as you are. We see the desire to administer wealth, your reason and your reaction. Facilitations of wealth in increments will be fashioned in your reality soon. Adonai, Dear One, I remain Saint Germain of the Violet Flame.

January 28, 2016 Thursday 9:30 a.m.

The I AM Presence of your nature is most present when you are teaching. More opportunities to teach through your vehicle will be arranged as you have agreed. The reason for giving, others an opportunity to contribute to the building fund, is for the purpose of their service opportunity to their soul's growth. You have an issue about asking for assistance personally and with acceptance. This issue comes from many years of feeling less worthy than others and learning to "make do" with what is available for your use. The value of your service is not registering in your emotional and mental bodies. You feel unsupported by us. You feel people do not really understand who you are and the service you perform in making your vehicle available to us and the Federation. Your ego is fighting the truth of your being. Adonai, Dear One, I remain Saint Germain.

January 29, 2016 Friday 9:30 a.m.

The reason for delay depends on the consciousness of the owners of the property as well as your own consciousness. Appropriate action: the letter to be distributed will move the energy into further manifestation. Timing in your dimension is not related to ours. We accommodate when possible your demand for expediency, but this is not always in alignment with the Divine Plan. Be well; be patient, calm and receptive. I remain Saint Germain of the Violet Flame.

January 30, 2016 Saturday 9:30 a.m.

It is important for Humanity to now know the availability and use of the Violet Flame of Transmutation, its uses and Powers, as well as the Sacred Fire Flame in the heart of every individual. You can cause this information to move around the World through the use of the Internet and email. Think of it as a positive virus to cause an epidemic of healing and transmutation of negativity and chaos. The choice is left to Humanity to participate in the Resurrection of Light and Freedom. Each individual's Freewill activates their desire to be whole and at one with Source, the Creator, and in tune with their own soul. Free will, the gift of Freewill from the Creator of Humanity can control or free an individual life stream from suffering through a choice to use the available Violet Flame of Freedom and Transmutation. Calling forth the Flame only requires intention, active decreeing and attention. Adonai, Dear One, I remain your servant Saint Germain.

January 31, 2016 Sunday 9:34 a.m.

Irrational thoughts are rampant in the minds and emotions of Humans as they take in an attempt to assimilate what they are being offered through the media. They have thus far not been offered truth: truth of the Spiritual Hierarchy, the Masters of this Universe, Angels, the members of the Intergalactic Federation. Your mission as you have accepted it is to make these truths available to the masses in several different forms. The Namaste Mystery School lessons are a big start on this project as are the materials about the Rays, their Masters and their uses. The connection to Connie Shaw and Jim is multi-purpose for receiving the gazing and for making the Ray information available to a wider audience. Think of more ways to distribute these truths as we will be making suggestions and appreciate the technical assistance of your dear daughter, Kelley. Adonai, Dear One, I remain Saint Germain, your friend, confidant and champion.

February 1, 2016 Monday 9:30 a.m.

Influence from higher dimensional beings is granted to those who expect and accept. Worthiness is not as considered as dedication to the Cause of Freedom to each individual life stream. The Cause of Freedom, my mission, also involves freeing the minds of Humans from the deceit they have been fed by those in charge in your dimension of the media and religion. Truth is rare in your reality.

As you read the books I have brought to you and as your Human mind attempts to expand to include the diversity and enormity of the work, progressing multi-dimensionally to attempt to wake up Humanity to even a small amount of truth that the underdeveloped Human mind can compre-hend is huge. We will need to begin slowly to open their hearts and minds to the truth.

Recently a few of the Universal Laws have been taught and exploited by books and teachings on manifestation – the Law of Attraction and the Law of Magnetism. The true Law of Soul Cooperation to assume the qualities necessary to become the vehicle through which the soul and I AM Presence are available in the Human unit is what is actually required as the goal, which is set before each Human.

To learn the Law of Energy Mastery must come before any other achieve-ment. The Law of Surrender of the vehicle to the soul and I AM Presence and willingness to listen, follow and achieve actively the will of the soul through the vehicle. You are an example of full surrender; however your Human mind still questions the reasons behind some of the suggestions of your soul. This is normal and not a judgment.

Take care of the physical body so that it is usable by the soul and the Spiritual Hierarchy you now serve. Conditioning limits what you have thus far been able to believe. Take time to ponder possibilities, ultimately releasing the methods and outcome to the Higher Will. Adonai, I remain Saint German, your friend and confidant.

February 3, 2016 Wednesday 9:32 a.m.

The study of the book Wired for Joy by Lauel Mellin will help you to un-derstand brain states as well as to understand your early programming or wiring. You were not unconditionally accepted nor did you live in a truly protected environment. When one lives in an environment where trust cannot be trusted the body, mind and spirit suffer erosion. The conscious mind is always searching for a safe place to be. You survived by shutting down and separating yourself from situations where you felt you could be judged or harmed. You sought solace in solitude only allowing intimacy in certain quarters. You did not understand the emotional pain of others or your own emotional pain, you only sought relief, which is what you thought the Valium would give you. You truly desired oblivion and felt others delib-erately caused you pain.

The memories are still in the body and brain wiring. Caution must be used when approaching any situation that is new or any situation of possible rejection. The circumstances are not under your control, your reactions are. Try to understand how you are feeling and take time to reference your past reactions in similar situations. The home you were renting prior to this one served your needs emotionally and physically at the time. Now you must decide what serves that need or desire and why and believe you are worthy and capable of maintaining your own security from inside yourself. You have proven this to yourself repeatedly. Know outer circumstances may change, but inner security can remain.

(I do know this. I have experienced it. It is just that change of residence and a circumstance always seems so inconvenient.) Yes, and inconvenience requires focus and commitment to a broader vision. Adonai, Dear One, I remain Saint Germain your confidant and champion.

8.

Saint Germain's Channeling On Mysticism

The mystic knows and understands their Soul created the body for the Soul's use in the physical dimension to further the Divine Plan for Earth, Humanity and all life on the Earth. A few will be willing to commit to the program. Do not attempt to convince anyone to attend this class.

Believing in a Higher Power is the first step in becoming a mystic. To understand that evolution of Earth and Humans and all species of life on Earth and beyond is an ongoing and continuous process is mandatory for a mystic and to also understand that Humans have the power to be self-evolving by choice.

It is the goal of a mystic to understand their individualized part to play within this evolution. When one understands themselves and their position within the Cosmic Big Picture, smaller events, collective events seem less worrisome and are better understood as that which is pushing evolution and causing these changes. While evolution is not always comfortable it can be comforting if viewed from the context of the Divine Plan of evolution not just of Humanity and animals, but of the Earth itself. The Earth is evolving and will evolve regardless of Humanity and Humanity's possible resistance to evolving spiritually.

All is happening at once in all dimensions and realities; evolution is a must. Your time is important, your consciousness is important to the Divine Plan of the Creator. Your evolution is assured. You notice it when you review your history as you write your own story evolution becomes obvious.

Often the suggestions from your soul have seemed far-fetched or as if it has nothing to do with progress or production. You are big on production while we in Spirit are big on progress. Production does not always mean or lead to soul progress and sometimes what is asked of you is not about your progress, but the progress of someone around you, or for someone we ask you to write to or to phone. It all makes sense from here, even the instantaneous change in plans. For we are seeing a mosaic of potential events potential connections and opportunities of which you are unaware. Flexibility and willingness to change directions, to change plans, is extremely important for one who chooses to follow the mystic path.

Be aware of timing, when to attempt what, and willingness to stop one chore or event to take the body to another location or to stop to make a suggested phone call or email or to post a letter. All has an order and rhythm within the Divine Plan.

Feeling adequate to any situation is the mark of a mystic who knows that it is the energy of the Infinite Wisdom, which can do all things through a Human consciousness, one that connects itself to its Source. True mysticism is giving in to the flow of Source energy through the body and mind of Cosmic Consciousness. To request, to desire this level of service to the Source, to Earth and Humanity is to desire to participate actively and consciously in the Divine Plan of the Creator of All That Is.

When an individual grows into this commitment the Universe rejoices as one joins the Company of Heaven to bring order, harmony and wisdom to Human consciousness. With the backing of All That Is one can give up fear, doubt and all confusion regarding decisions, directions and outcomes. All is well and will be well when one chooses constant contact with their Source, their Soul.

Changing an attitude about wealth is necessary for a mystic. Mysticism reflects the goodness, opulence and wealth-generosity of the Source of all Creation. To accept that you are an aspect of the Source embodied as a Human is the first step to wealth and Oneness. To understand the availability of wealth, not just on Earth, but also in other dimensions is a sign of understanding All That Is as Oneness. To separate one's consciousness from wealth takes effort and disbelief in Oneness. A being is either conscious of Oneness or they are not. When Oneness is achieved by Human Consciousness enlightenment is achieved.

You are waffling between Oneness and separation in your consciousness. You want to believe, you do believe in the certainty of God, but not so much in the certainty of your Selfhood as Divine. (How do I change this?) Through affirmation: I Am an aspect of God operating through my personality for the benefit of Earth, all species of life on the Earth and beyond.

Correct definition of self and understanding the soul created the body for its use begins cooperation between the personality and the soul. The will of the individual is not taken away when the individual allows the soul consciousness access to the body, but furthers the heart's desires of the individual by conscious co-creation of events and opportunities. The will of the Soul does not override the will of the individual. If the desire of the individual is coming from the ego rather than the heart the soul can modify opportunities and events to bring this differentiation to the conscious attention of the individual. The will of the soul is aligned with the original contract of the portion of the consciousness assigned to the body before incarnation. The contracts are mutable and can be extended or made more elaborate by the individual consciousness. Usually when the body consciousness deliberately and intentionally invites the conscious participation of the soul into the body and life stream, the contract is expanded from being simply a karmic contract with one's family and friends from other life times to a more worthy planetary contract, which involves the Earth, Humanity and all life on the Earth and beyond.

At this point the body consciousness comes in contact with either a Master in meditation or a physical teacher who has accomplished this connection. Through this connection the body consciousness will learn of and begin to have experiences of the Spiritual Hierarchy, the Intergalactic Federation and Angels. These connections or thoughts that these beings exist can be mentally conceptualized by the individual before the soul contact and commitment is made, but are only intellectual thought forms and do not actually bring about actual contact with these other realms. When one deliberately begins to communicate with their soul and a Master they are made privy to their place and responsibility within the Divine Plan and are expected to take an active role in working with the Spiritual Hierarchy. This work is not for everyone and must happen from a point of choice by the individual.

Mysticism as a path requires first the inner desire to surrender suffering, confusion, guilt, doubt, shame and fear. It requires a commitment to accept knowingness and release excuses. It requires self-observation and self-responsibility and the ability to respond to the true Self, the Higher Self, the soul. It requires allowing the Soul to negotiate with the egoic beliefs, attitudes and desires. It requires releasing the need to be right, to be popular, and to be thought of as smart or successful by others. To be willing to be guided by suggestions coming from the soul is necessary.

To be a mystic does not remove an individual's Freewill. A mystic chooses not to react to outside influences, but chooses to respond from the level of the Soul's suggestion.

Confusion in the Human mind is caused by fear of the Truth. Confusion or the excuse of confusion "not knowing" comes from unwillingness to know truth. When confused a being only has to expect to know, expect the solution to be there in the mind to replace confusion. In the absolute, one always knows in the abstract lies confusion of warring factions of the ego self, which desires to reign through confusing the conscious mind. Solutions are always available from the Soul, the Holy Christ Self if one ceases to accept the state of confusion and enters into silence where the solutions reside.

Negative thought forms from the collective impinge upon the important messages attempting to be communicated to Humans from their souls. This is why your work and the work of others to use the Violet Flame for the clearing of the density of negative thought forms are so important.

To truly receive this service of direct information coming to one from other dimensions there must be no fear in the individual about what information will be transmitted and the individual must be willing to perceive the information as not being "made up" by their imagination. To truly communicate with us only takes intention, willingness and cooperation. It does not involve giving over one's will or in any way allowing another being to overtake a person's body; only the energetic connection is necessary through the terminal of your brain frequency. The idea of creating, installing through intention, what we've called a gatekeeper at your highest level of consciousness to censor a person being approached by an impersonating consciousness is a worthwhile system, because there are many in lower dimensions, the astral plane, who would and could take advantage of an open channel to speak and communicate information that sounds truthful but is fabricated by that entity with the express intention of feeding on the host's consciousness, energy and body and on any bodies the host convinces to listen to the messages coming from such an over-riding consciousness.

May 8, 2016 Sunday 9:18 a.m.

Teaching mysticism is the higher calling for many at this time. The need for teachers who have accepted the path of the mystic for themselves will be the dominant focus of the Spiritual Hierarchy for this Aquarian Age. To attune Humans to the Divine aspect of their creation and consciousness is *a requirement of this Age of evolution of the Human species. For a politician to admit their belief in God is an anathema to political success. This must change. Those of you who are conscious have a responsibility to acknowledge this need and to promote energetically into the political system of all governments and particularly into American politics this consideration into the hearts and minds of candidates. Use your ability to focus and project thought to accomplish this mission. The future of America and the Earth depends on the survival and function of your ability to perform this service.*

May 9, 2016 Monday 9:15 a.m.

Working with the consciousness of the candidates for the office of president and vice-president of America is an imperative assignment. Without this intervention the outcome can be retarding for America and the World. Integrity is a must for anyone holding these offices. Their integrity needs to come under scrutiny and exposure of past inconsistencies revealed. Do this with energy and intention. Use the Violet Flame and the illumination of the Christ vibration. Call upon the assistance of the Saturn Command to shine the light of exposure into anything that is out of integrity within the American government.

Adonai, Dear Ones, I remain Saint Germain of the Violet Flames of Transmutation and Freedom, your advocate and friend.

3-6-17

[The Earth is now in the Fourth dimension headed for the Fifth. This information relates to the Hierarchy's plan to arrange for more people to ascend with the Earth.]

When a person first leaves their body through physical death they are grateful to find they still exist. They become aware quickly that their thoughts create their reality and create instantly some pretty crazy and somewhat horrifying events. They are met by masters or higher vibrational beings shortly after their arrival. The being's vibration when they left their body affects where they show up in their afterlife or, more accurately, their between life, because very few Humans develop and prepare themselves, while still in their bodies, not to have a need to return to Earth to further their commitment to their soul contract for that life.

They are taken to a way station and supported by Guardians to make decisions about what to explore while they are between Earth lives and what to study to better understand the Law of One before they commit to their next Human life.

Currently, now that the alternative Earth (Ploarus) is established and filled with life supporting atmosphere, plants, animals and minerals, only a few higher level beings will be qualified to reincarnate on the original Earth. Most people leaving their Earth bodies now are only vibrationally qualified to reincarnate on the alternative Third dimensional Earth to have an opportunity to learn Love and the Laws governing all things.

As the Earth ascends, those who qualify vibrationally to move with the Earth into the Fifth dimension will be retained. The "harvest" as it is called in upper dimensions is what has been previously referred to biblically as separating the wheat from the chaff.

Those soul aspects that you have convinced to descend from higher regions to help rescue more Humans who are, as we might say, on the border or the fence about doing the spiritual work to learn about truth and the Spiritual Law will become escalated in their desire to seek truth and to raise their vibrations through meditation, exercise, nutrients, giving up addictions and their negative thoughts and intentions.

We are enthusiastic that this project will make a huge difference in speeding up the time line for the ascension of Earth. Many will be able to ascend after their physical body death if they raise their vibrations now. Many Humans that have been on the fence so to speak about committing to their soul's path hopefully will commit. <u>In my night work I have been assigned to recruit higher level soul</u> aspects to over light Humans currently in body to reach the goal of shifting into the Fifth dimension. The goal set by the Hierarchy was to recruit one billion aspects to over light by the end of 2017. The first wave was 2,500 on December 12, 2016 when the project began. The second wave brought us to January 8, 2017 and we had 6,000,000 volunteers at that time.

It has grown weekly from then to:
Jan. 10, 2017 - 6,391,000
Jan.11, 2017 - 6,963,000
Jan. 23, 2017 - 9,627,000
Jan. 27, 2017 - 10,765,000
Jan.29, 2017 - 12,964,000
Feb. 8, 2017 - 25, 963,000
Feb. 11, 2017 - 26, 240,000

Feb. 12, 2017 - 29, 267,000
Feb. 14, 2017 - 31,946,210
Feb. 16, 2017 - 32,675, 826
Feb. 22, 2017 - 40,264,852
Feb. 26, 2017 - 52,745,010
March 2, 2017 - 53,675,240
March 12, 2017 - 71,254,760
March 19, 2017 - 82,967,522
March 27, 2017 - 91,364,029

Saint Germain has reported to me that the soul aspects will be monitored to see what progress is made by each soul. I was concerned that this monitoring would also be my job, but fortunately it has been assigned to another group. He did say this morning: "You will not be required to maintain these aspects; your only responsibility was to make the request, explain the need and to record your request for distribution into all dimensions from 5th to 9th. We are ahead of any projection we had established for this event and now feel our projection of one billion for this year was low; and we now believe it would not be unrealistic to hold the vision for 3 to 5 billion souls to upgrade by December 2017. Our first projection involved one billion souls making the shift to the Fifth dimension possible for Earth by the end of 2017. Adonai, Dear One."

Channeling 3-26-17 From Saint Germain

Your focus on the after life of a Human or more accurately between lives of Humans is intensely important at this time because as the harvest proceeds more and more Humans will not be returning to Earth, so reincarnation of the Human species as it has been experienced here-to-fore, will vary with a few returning to Earth as you know it and more moving to reside on the alternative Earth. You might imagine that for the current Earth to take its rightful place within the galaxy war and violence cannot continue.

This harvesting of souls and relocation of souls unwilling to wake up will be progressive and will take years to be fully accomplished. The pressures of higher vibrational soul aspects joining current Human bodies will, in a vibrational or energetic sense, force or enforce spiritual evolution.

The Earth and Humanity have gone as far as is allowed by Spiritual Law before a cleansing can happen through cataclysmic events or through saturation of higher consciousness into Human forms. The process of saturation has been chosen over cataclysmic events as much to protect the Earth from physical destruction by Human unconscious activity, i.e. war and violence. These actions must be transformed or transferred from Earth for Earth's evolution to take place. Earth's transition into the Fifth dimension is more vital than Human evolution on Earth; Human evolution can be reseeded on the alternative Earth. The Earth cannot withstand more violence and destruction and Earth's evolution is vital to the evolution of your galaxy and the Universe.

You will wake up with the over lighting aspects coming in now. Adonai

THE MASTERS May 21, 2019

Bringing together a group such as this and those who came for the weekend serves their souls and those of us who serve continually. When such an event happens, we join together out efforts with those members of the Federation who serve to further educate Humans in Oneness and as aspects of Divinity. As they disburse to their own residence you will all be disbursed, but not disbanded. The links between you have greatly solidified now to retain telepathic communion through intention. Coming from diverse backgrounds you all bring functions to play throughout the Universe into other civilizations as well as other races and civilizations on your Earth.

Being consciously multi-dimensional will become the norm and it will assist you all to better grasp and function within the Human matrix of Earth as well as joining together to participate consciously with us and the members of the Federation.

Adonai, Dear One.

www.ingramcontent.com/pod-product-compliance
Lightning Source LLC
Chambersburg PA
CBHW021345090426
42742CB00008B/755